Sue Emery
Gill Mackie
Nicholas Stephens

Intermediate

NEW EDITIONS

Contents

Contents

A Who do you think lives in these houses? Match the people to the houses.

Reading Link

B Read the article through quickly and explain the title.

MANCHESTER ~ A Tale of Two Cities

Stephen Nickson comes back with a surprising report after his visit to a city in the North of England.

1

The sale of a riverside flat in Manchester for £1 million a few weeks ago shows that the heart of the city is becoming popular with the rich. But that doesn't mean that the whole of Manchester is getting wealthier. Just three kilometres from the luxury flat in Century Buildings lies Jubilee Street, where residents live in damp, old houses which sell for only £7,000.

2

Just fifteen years ago, there wasn't much difference in house prices in the central Manchester area. Now, the difference is enormous.

House developers, *Urban Splash*, are now changing an old factory into flats which will sell for up to £750,000. 'Nobody could sell flats for this price four years ago,' says Tom Bloxham, who owns *Urban Splash*. 'But now people are queuing up for them.'

3

It's not surprising that the flats like those in Century Buildings are both spacious and luxurious. With their iced-glass floors, luxury bathrooms and electronic systems for controlling temperature and lighting, they are attracting international businessmen and women. 'Now, for the first time, people can find good quality housing in the centre of Manchester,' says Mr Nesbit of *Blue Sapphire* estate agents, who were responsible for selling the flats in Century Buildings. 'Even the views compare well with the best areas of London.'

4

One thing the residents will not see from their apartments is Samantha Green's council house.

Samantha is a 35-year-old single mother of five. Their house is damp and too cramped for six people, and she wants to move for health reasons. 'My eldest son, Gary, is eighteen and he's got backache at the moment. Jody – who's six – has a bad cold. Someone is always sick,' she says.

5

Samantha's house and the flats in Century Buildings may be worlds apart but everyone in central Manchester shares a fear of crime. Fortunately for the wealthier residents, the problem has been partly solved by good security.

Samantha, though, is not so lucky. 'I rarely go out at night and I feel like a prisoner in my own home after dark. But that's the way things are when you're poor, isn't it?' she says, looking towards the river.

C Now read the article again and match these headings with each part (1-5).

A A world of difference
B A common problem
C The other side of the coin
D Great changes
E An ideal home

Vocabulary Link

D These words and phrases are in the article. Circle the closest meaning for each one.

1 residents (part 1)	a	people who live in a place
	b	poor people
2 enormous (part 2)	a	very different
	b	very big
3 queuing up (part 2)	a	waiting for
	b	making a line
4 attracting (part 3)	a	making people interested
	b	becoming more beautiful
5 worlds apart (part 5)	a	near to each other
	b	completely different

E Find these adjectives in the text and write them in the table. Add two more positive and negative words of your own.

cramped spacious damp luxurious

Positive	Negative

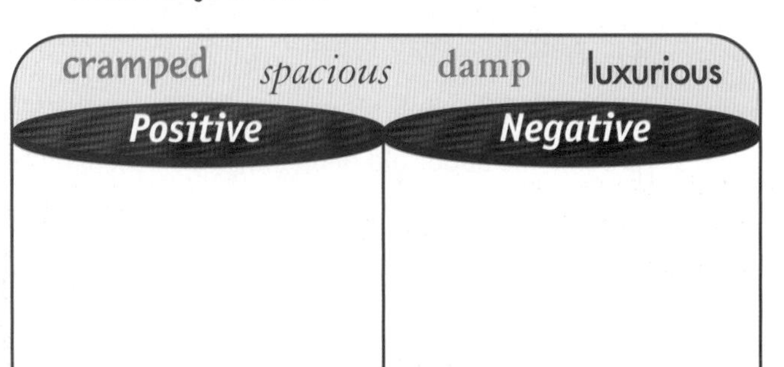

F Use the word given in capitals at the end of each sentence to form a word that fits in the space. All the words are in the article.

HINTS

Think about the kind of word that is needed:

- Does it describe a noun? It's probably an adjective.
- Does it tell us how something is done? It's an adverb.
- Does it come after an adjective or article? It's probably a noun.

1 It's not my fault! I'm not .... for the living arrangements. ***RESPONSIBILITY***

2 All .... should make sure that they lock the door when they leave. ***RESIDE***

3 What's the .... between a terraced house and a detached house? A terraced house has other houses on each side, but a detached house stands by itself. ***DIFFERENT***

4 Most students who come to live in London prefer a .... location. ***CENTRE***

5 People who live in big cities are very worried about the increase in .... ***CRIMINAL***

6 The Docklands area of London became .... with rich young people in the 1980s. ***POPULARITY***

7 The .... of the old house was a big surprise; nobody in their right mind would want to live there! ***SELL***

8 Some parents are concerned about their children's .... ***HEALTHY***

Grammar Link

Present Simple, Present Continuous, Adverbs of Frequency

Look at the tense used in these examples.

*..., where residents **live** in damp, old houses which **sell** for only £7,000.*

*I rarely **go out** at night ...*

Look at the tense used here.

*... they **are attracting** international businessmen and women.*

*But now people **are queuing up** for them.*

Complete the following rules.

The .... tense is used to talk about things which are true in general.

The .... tense is used to talk about how often something happens.

The .... tense is used to talk about actions that are in progress at or around the time of speaking.

Remember

Stative verbs are not used in the Present Continuous tense. See the Grammar Reference on page 100.

Look at the position of the adverbs in these examples.

*I **rarely** go out at night ...*
*Someone is **always** sick ...*

Complete the following rule.

We use an adverb of frequency to say how .... something happens. It comes .... the verb in the Present Simple. When we use the verb **be**, we put the adverb .... the verb.

Do you know any other adverbs of frequency? Make a list and then check with the list in the Grammar Reference on page 100.

....
....
....
....

G Put the verbs in brackets into the correct form and put the adverbs of frequency in the correct position, where necessary.

1 The architects .... (never be) here when you want them.
2 He .... (get) ready to start a new project at the moment.
3 My father .... (always go) to bed before midnight.
4 Amy .... (not often visit) her grandmother.
5 They .... (cut) the grass now.
6 .... (you paint) your house every year?

Listening Link

H Listen to these parts of conversations where people are speaking in different situations. Choose which answer is correct from **a**, **b** or **c**.

HINTS

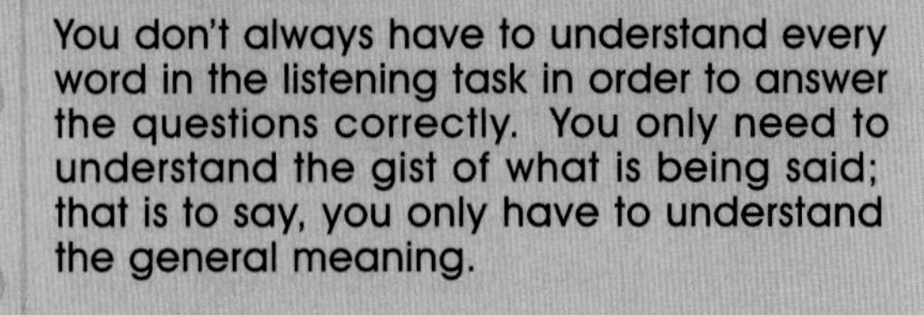
You don't always have to understand every word in the listening task in order to answer the questions correctly. You only need to understand the gist of what is being said; that is to say, you only have to understand the general meaning.

1 You overhear a man talking to a friend on his mobile phone. What is he complaining about?
   a his new neighbours' music
   b the state of his new house
   c the dull wallpaper

2 You hear a woman talking to a friend on the bus. What is her problem?
   a She is afraid to leave her house.
   b She is sick because the house is old.
   c She cannot get any help with the rent.

3 You overhear a man and a woman talking in a shop. What are they doing?
   a choosing some new furniture
   b looking at carpets and curtains
   c getting a chair repaired

4 You hear two women talking on a television programme about old people living on the streets. What are they worried about?
   a their health
   b their relationships
   c not having food

Grammar Link

Question Tags

Look at this question taken from the article.

But that's the way things are when you're poor, ***isn't it?***

How do you form a question tag? ....

....

Complete the following rule.

We use a .... question tag with a positive sentence and a .... question tag with a negative sentence.

Study the Grammar Reference on page 100 before you do the task.

I Make questions by putting question tags on the end of the following sentences.

1. We are going home soon, ...?
2. She doesn't like me, ...?
3. It isn't too far away, ...?
4. They've fixed the locks, ...?
5. You have to work late today, ...?

Speaking Link

J In pairs, ask and answer these questions.

- Where do you live?
- What improvements could be made to your area?
- Where would your ideal home be?
- Do you spend a lot of time at home?
- What is your home like?
- What is your favourite room like?

HINTS

When you answer questions in English, use the same tense as the question:

Where do you live?
I live in London.

Try not to answer with just a 'yes' or 'no'. Explain why you feel the way you do, or give details or examples.

Writing Link

K *Imagine that you have moved house and that you now live in another town. Your best friend gave you a present before you left, and you want to write a letter to thank him/her.*

Complete the letter with the expressions below. There may be more than one possibility.

Helpful Expressions

- **a** Keep in touch.
- **b** Write soon.
- **c** I'm writing to thank you for ...
- **d** Thanks again for the ...
- **e** I'm sorry I didn't write sooner, ...
- **f** Thanks a lot for the ....

Dear Sandy

How are you? (1) ...... but I was waiting for my dad to connect my computer in my new room.
(2) ...... the pen you gave me.
It's great. I know I use the computer a lot, but I still have to write at school. I'm going to keep the pen especially for the exams.

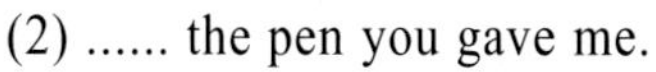

The new house is really big and so David and I have our own rooms. That means you can visit and stay in my room because there are two beds. The house is close to the town centre so there are lots of things for us to do.

So, (3) ...... pen and lots of love to your mum and dad. (4) ...... I hope to see you soon.

love

Emma

L Now write a letter to your friend, thanking him/her for the present, and telling him/her about your new house and area. (80-100 words)

Letter Outline

Greeting	Dear (Sandy)
Paragraph 1	Say why you are writing.
Paragraph 2	Give details about your new house and the area it is in.
Closing paragraph	Thank your friend again.
Signing off	Love / Best wishes (Emma)

A Which of the following do you think will help you most to choose a career?

parents
teachers
money
friends
relatives

B Match these words with the jobs shown in the photographs.

C Read the article through quickly and explain how Ashley Judd is different from most other actors.

ON THE WAY UP

Ashley Judd is a rising star in Hollywood, but what is she really like?

One characteristic that an actor usually needs is good looks, and Ashley Judd IS very pretty. Hollywood actresses, though, are not usually famous for being brainy. Ashley has both beauty and brains and is proud of her success at the University of Kentucky.

Ashley was born in San Francisco in 1969. Her father left soon after she was born and her mother was a struggling singer who moved so often that Ashley went to twelve different schools in thirteen years. When she was sixteen, her mum and sister signed a contract with a large record company. They sold 15 million albums, which made Ashley 'famous' while she was still studying at school. She was always independent and wanted to be an actor rather than follow in her mother's footsteps.

After leaving university, she went to Los Angeles and found work in television. Then came roles in *Ruby in Paradise*, *A Time to Kill* and *Smoke and Heat*. She stayed in LA until 1993 when her house burnt down. After that she decided to live in an old farmhouse just outside Nashville, Tennessee, which is unusual since most Hollywood actors live in LA.

Ashley believes that living in the country protects her from the negative side of fame. But her country girl image is not the only one she wants people to see. She looks elegant in designer clothes and always surprises people by supporting her ideas with references to what she has read and studied, (which, in Hollywood, is unusual).

Her short wavy black hair and large, sleepy eyes may not say much about her, but her manner certainly does. She realises that she will have to become very famous to get everything she dreams about.

Her roles in *Ruby in Paradise* and *Double Jeopardy* are those of people who are very independent and prefer to spend their time alone. Major film stars often turn down such roles, but Ashley made up her mind to accept both roles as she was reading the scripts.

Vocabulary Link

E The words and phrases below have been taken from the article. Circle the word or phrase closest in meaning to each one.

1	brainy (para 1)	a clever b difficult to control
2	struggling (para 2)	a having difficulties b successful
3	contract (para 2)	a agreement b cheque
4	follow in her mother's footsteps (para 2)	a use her mother's shoes b do the same thing as her mother
5	image (para 4)	a reflection in a mirror b the way someone is seen by others
6	manner (para 5)	a the way someone behaves b the things somebody says

D Now read the article carefully and choose the best answer **a**, **b**, **c** or **d** for each of the questions (1-4).

1 When did Ashley's life as a teenager change?
- a when she was 13 years old
- b when she became more independent
- c as soon as she left home
- d when her mother became successful

2 In 1993, Ashley
- a went to Los Angeles.
- b moved to Hollywood.
- c had to move house.
- d decided to leave Nashville.

3 What does *one* in paragraph 4 refer to?
- a her success
- b her farmhouse
- c her fame
- d her image

4 How could Ashley Judd best be described?
- a unsociable and critical
- b intelligent and determined
- c dull and boring
- d shy and lonely

F Add **-er**, **-or**, **-ist** or **-ian** to the words below to make the names of some jobs. Some changes must be made to some of the words. Then put the jobs into the table.

act art bank
design engine law music
politics teach wait

Creative	Friendly	Organised

G Tick (✓) the boxes to show which words can go with the verbs.

arrange	find	make	write	
				a book
				a cheque
				a letter
				a meeting
				a mistake
				a telephone call
				work

Grammar Link

Past Simple, Past Continuous

Look at the tense used in these examples.

*... Ashley **went** to twelve different schools in thirteen years.*

*When she **was** sixteen, her mum and sister **signed** a contract ...*

Look at the tense used here.

*... while she **was** still **studying** at school.*

Find another sentence like this in the text.

....

Which tense often follows **while** and **as**?

....

Complete the following rules.

The .... tense is used to talk about a state or a completed action in the past when the time is important.

The .... tense describes an action that was in progress at a certain time in the past.

See page 112 for a list of irregular verbs. Study the Grammar Reference on page 101 before you do the task.

H Put the verb in brackets into either the Past Simple or the Past Continuous forms.

1. While I .... (use) my computer, I .... (hear) a strange noise.
2. The salesman .... (walk) up the steps, ... (ring) the bell and .... (wait).
3. The burglar .... (break in) while Bob .... (work) on his car in the garage.
4. She .... (give) me the keys to the new office as I .... (get) ready to leave.
5. .... (you write) to her while she .... (work) abroad?
6. We .... (not notice) anything unusual while we .... (check) the morning post.

Listening Link

I You will hear part of an interview with a teenager who wants to act in a film for young people. Fill in the missing information in part of the interviewer's form.

HINTS

In some listening tasks you are expected to write down some of the facts and figures you hear. In these cases, you should listen very carefully for the FINAL confirmation of a number, date, day, etc. Don't be in a hurry to write down the first thing you hear.

Past Experience

Last role ***Emily in 'The First Rain in Manchester'***

Number of years		
singing		*8*
dancing	**(1)**	
horse-riding		*4*

Date available to start rehearsals **(2)** ....

Previous fee **(3)** ....

Date of issue of Equity Card **(4)** ....

Place of issue ***Lambeth Walk, London***

Speaking Link

J Look at the two photographs below. Describe them, saying what is different and what is similar about them. You can use the expressions below to help you.

Both photographs show ... .

In picture A ..., but in picture B ... .

The people in the first photo ..., while the person in the second photo ... .

A

flames, fire hose, helmet, equipment, burning building

B

astronaut, space, spacesuit, float, spacecraft

- Would you like to do either of these jobs?
- Why/Why not?
- Which job is more dangerous/exciting?

Writing Link

K Read the composition below which describes one of the people in picture A (Speaking Link).

Alan Pearson is a tall, well-built fire fighter in his early thirties. He followed in his father's footsteps when he left school fifteen years ago.

Fire fighting, as you can imagine, is both exciting and dangerous. In one rescue, Alan nearly died because of a problem with his breathing equipment. Luckily, he managed to get himself and the children he was rescuing to safety before he lost consciousness.

When he is not working, Alan likes parachuting. His favourite pastime, however, is rather surprising: he loves painting portraits.

Although Alan has received many awards for his bravery, he says 'I'm just doing my job.' I believe that more people should appreciate the risks Alan takes.

L Complete the composition outline with **a**, **b**, **c** and **d**.

Composition Outline

Paragraph 1	☐	**Paragraph 3**	☐
Paragraph 2	☐	**Paragraph 4**	☐

a Finish off the composition by saying what you think of the person you are describing.

b Describe the person's job and give details of his/her most exciting moment.

c Describe the person's appearance and mention his/her job.

d Describe what the person does in his/her free time, and say if you think his/her hobbies are surprising.

M *Now write a description of someone whose job you would like to do.*

Use the outline and remember to think of details and examples to make the person sound real. You could write about the person in picture B. (80-100 words)

A Discuss these questions with a friend.

- Have you ever been banned from doing anything either at home or at school? Why?
- What kind of things are you allowed/ not allowed to do?
- What do you think teenagers should be able to do in your country?

Reading Link

B Read through the leaflet quickly to find out what mistake a large record chain made.

DISCO RIGHTS

Do you want other people to tell you what music to listen to? *1* We're holding a special disco party for all teenagers in the area and we're going to sign a petition for Channel 9's *Midnight Shock Show* to get our DJ and our music back.

Background

Last Thursday, police arrested DJ Cat-B at Channel 9's studios for playing music they thought was not suitable for young people. As the police were arresting him, Cat-B said, '*2* I'll make sure that all the kids who listen to my show get a chance to protest against this.'

Music Censorship

There are two ways of banning music: either the government can ban a record or an individual person or organisation can do so. The government will usually ban music if they can show that it has no serious social, artistic, literary or scientific value. *3* However, when an individual wants to ban something, according to the law, he or she can do this for any reason. This means that your parents, your teachers or your neighbours can ban anything they like if they believe it's not good for you.

Famous Bans

- In 1955, rock music stations in Chicago were not allowed to play any rhythm and blues music.
- In 1957, the camera crew on *The Ed Sullivan Show* could only film the top half of Elvis Presley because of the way he danced.
- In 1966, the Beatles were in trouble and had records banned because John Lennon upset some religions with his comments. They also had to change the cover of one of their records.
- In 1971, officials tried to ban a whole list of popular music because they said the lyrics were about drugs. *4*
- In 1981, religious organisations successfully banned Olivia Newton John's hit *Physical*.
- In the nineties, a record chain made a big mistake when it stuck a notice on Frank Zappa's *Jazz from Hell* album. The sticker said that nobody under the age of 18 could buy the record because of the 'dirty lyrics'. All the tracks on the album were instrumental!

What happens next?

When Cat-B goes to court next month, he will take our petition with him to show the judge that young people want to hear the music he is playing on the radio show. We are sure he will win. So, let's hear your voice.

Space at the disco is unlimited. *5* Food will be hot. No alcohol or drugs are allowed on the premises.

C The leaflet you read had five gaps. Here are the missing sentences. Can you put them in the right place in the leaflet?

A This is a big mistake.

B One of the records was the children's song *Puff the Magic Dragon.*

C Music will be loud.

D If not, come and join the meeting at Hatter's Youth Club on Saturday, 8th May at 7.00 pm sharp!

E In fact, it is not the music that people ban, but the lyrics.

Vocabulary Link

D Here is a word map using words and phrases from the leaflet. Look at it carefully and see if you can complete it using the words given.

disco, Midnight Shock Show, Elvis Presley, Frank Zappa, cover, instrumental, lyrics, rhythm and blues, tracks

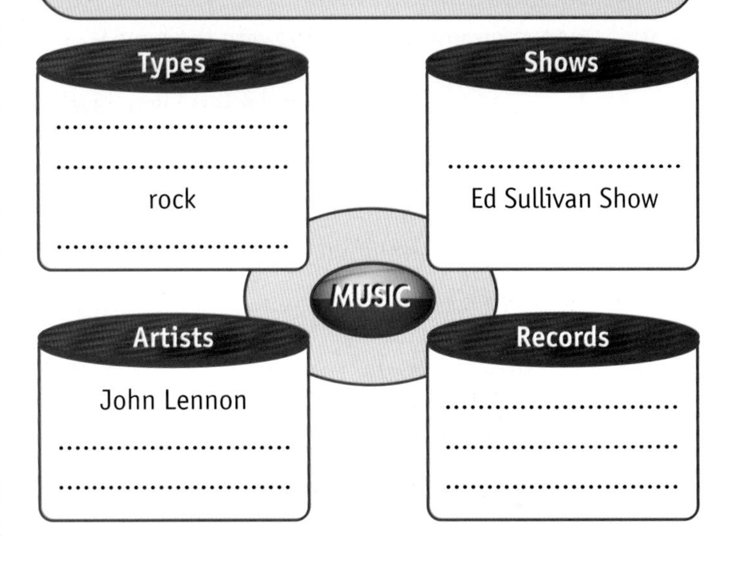

Now see if you can complete this map with different types of musical instruments.

bagpipes, bass guitar, organ, saxophone, synthesiser, tambourine, triangle, trumpet, violin

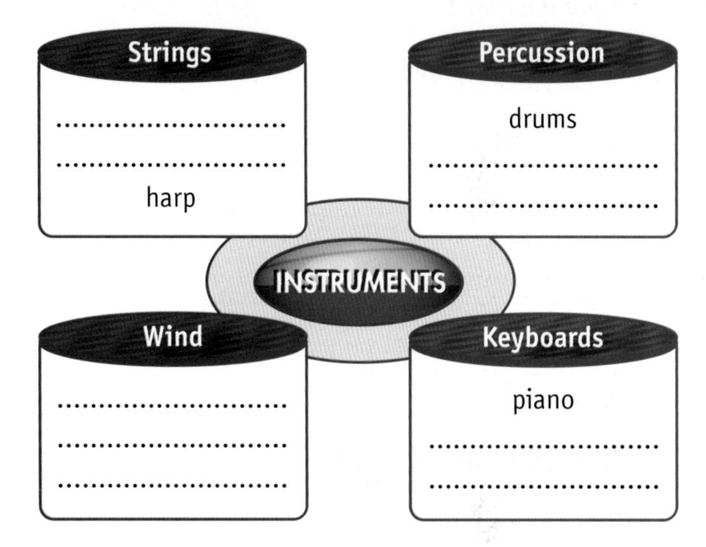

E Complete the sentences with the correct preposition. All the phrases are in the leaflet.

1 Do you think an electric guitar is a suitable birthday present .... a teenager who loves Heavy Metal music?

2 Did you hear that police arrested DJ Magic .... playing the latest Ozzy Ozbourne CD?

3 People under the age .... eighteen are not allowed in the jazz club.

4 According .... the latest research, very loud music can damage your hearing.

5 Mike's .... trouble again. The neighbours called the police because his band was playing in his garage after midnight.

6 Turn that music down! I'm sure it isn't good .... you!

F Match the verbs with the pictures and then write a sentence for each one.

1 look forward to ....

2 switch off ....

3 switch on ....

4 turn down ....

5 turn up ....

a ☐

b ☐

c ☐

d ☐

e ☐

Grammar Link

Future Simple, Present Continuous, be going to

Look at the tense used at the beginning of this example.

***I'll make sure** that all the kids who listen to my show get a chance to protest against this.*

Who is Cat-B making a promise to? ....
Who is he threatening? ....

Look at the tense used to make this prediction.

*We are sure he **will win**.*

Which tense is used below? ....

*We**'re holding** a special disco party for all teenagers ...*

Now read this example.

*... we**'re going to** sign a petition for Channel 9's Midnight Shock Show ...*

Why don't we use the Future Simple in these two sentences?
....

Complete the following rules.

The .... tense is used to make predictions, ... and threats.

The .... tense and .... can be used to talk about arrangements and plans that have been made for the future.

Remember

A future tense cannot be used in a future clause with **when**. You must use a present tense. Look at the example:

***When** Cat-B **goes** to court next month, ...*

Study the Grammar Reference on pages 101 and 102 before you do the task.

G Put the verbs in brackets into the correct form. Use the Future Simple, Present Continuous, Present Simple or *be going to*. More than one answer may be possible.

1. I .... (sing) you a song every day and that's a promise.
2. The group .... (phone) you when their lead singer .... (get back).
3. The bass guitarist and I .... (have) a meeting after lunch.
4. I .... (spend) next summer touring the islands with the band.
5. I .... (make sure) you never work for a circus again. You're finished!
6. There .... (be) another technological revolution in music in the next twenty years.
7. I .... (not tell) her what you said about her voice. I promise.
8. We .... (visit) the old music hall. Do you want to come?
9. When the audience .... (see) the magician's new act, they .... (be) amazed.
10. Bob and Carol .... (get) engaged next week, before they release their new album.

Listening Link

H You will hear three different people talking about musical instruments. Choose from the list (**a-d**) which instrument each speaker is interested in learning. Notice that there is an extra letter that you will not use.

a	flute	Speaker **1**	
b	drums	Speaker **2**	
c	violin	Speaker **3**	
d	saxophone		

HINTS

- In tasks where you have to match speakers to another piece of information, you will almost always find that speakers talk about similar experiences or facts. Therefore, you need to **check** before you write your answer.
- Remember that you might hear a synonym on the tape for the key word in the question.

Speaking Link 

I Imagine that your school has decided to hold a talent contest for the best school band. In pairs, talk to each other and make decisions about:

- Judges
- Prizes
- Host / Presenter
- Refreshments

You can use the expressions below to help you.

> I think / believe (that) ... because ... .
> What do you think about ... ?
> Do you agree?
> I agree with you up to a point, but ... .

Now report back to the class.
Did anybody have the same ideas as you?

Writing Link 

J *Imagine that you are organising the school talent contest. Look at the list and part of a letter from Mr Jones, who owns a record company that has offered to supply the prizes for the talent contest.*

Prizes	***for 1st, 2nd and 3rd place***
Judges	***one child from each year, chosen by their classmates***
Host/Presenter	***DJ from local radio station***

We would like to know more about your school talent contest. Could you tell us when and where you are planning to have the contest? It would also be very useful if we knew how many bands you expect to enter.

K Complete the letter opposite with the words and phrases below.

Helpful Expressions

a If you need anything else, I will be happy to help.
b Finally, ...
c I hope the following information will be helpful.
d Firstly, ...
e Regarding/Concerning...

Dear Mr Jones

Thank you for your letter asking about our school talent contest and offering to supply the prizes. ***1*** *.........*

2 *......... the contest will take place in the school gymnasium on Friday, 15th December at 7.30 pm. DJ Magic, from Radio XYZ, will be the host.* ***3*** *......... judges, the students have already voted for one judge from each year.* ***4*** *......... although about fifteen bands will take part, there will only be prizes for the first three places.*

I would like to thank you again for your kind offer. ***5*** *.........*

Yours sincerely

Sam Thompson

L Now write your letter to the record company, using the outline below and your ideas from the Speaking Link. (80-100 words)

Letter Outline

Greeting	Dear (Mr Jones)
Paragraph 1	Thank the reader for his/her offer and explain why you are writing.
Paragraph 2	Give the information you have been asked to give, in a logical order. Do not use exactly the same words as the question.
Closing paragraph	Thank the reader again for his/her offer. Say that you can answer any other questions he/she may have.
Signing off	Yours sincerely (Sam Thompson)

Unit 4 Fashion

A Discuss the following questions.

- What is in fashion at the moment?
- How long do things stay in fashion?
- What do you think people will say about today's clothes and footwear in ten or twenty years' time?

Reading Link

B Read the brochure quickly to find out where the art collection is kept.

These boots were made for walking – or were they?

A Introduction

Welcome to one of the largest collections of footwear in the world that will make you green with envy. Here at the *Footwear Museum* you can see exhibits from all over the world. You can find out about shoes, boots and sandals worn by everyone from the Ancient Egyptians to pop stars.

Did you know that the boots Neil Armstrong wore on the moon in 1969 were thrown away before he returned to earth, to make sure that they didn't bring back any germs?

B Room 1

The celebrity footwear section is probably the most popular in the entire museum. Started in the 1950s, there is a vast selection of shoes and boots belonging to everyone from queens and prime ministers to pop stars and actors! Most visitors find their choice of footwear fascinating.

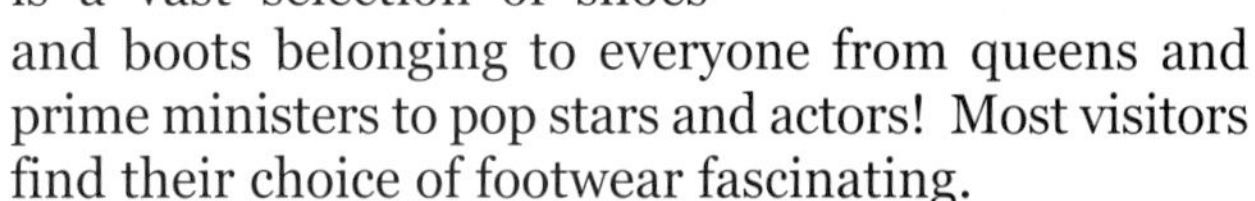

Did you know that Napoleon Bonaparte's servants had to wear his shoes to break them in before he would wear them?

C Room 2

Most of our visitors are amazed – and horrified – by the selection of *special purpose* shoes on display here at the Museum of Footwear. For example, there are Chinese shoes made of silk which were worn by women to bind their feet to prevent them from growing too much!

Did you know that women are four times more likely to have foot problems than men?

D Room 3

As well as shoes and boots, the museum also exhibits shoe-shaped objects. The variety is incredible. For example, there is a bronze lamp which resembles a pair of sandals, and Greek perfume bottles which look like legs!

Did you know that shoes were worn as early as 10,000 BC?

E The Footwear Library

People come from all over the world to study in our comprehensive footwear library. Designers and researchers come here to look up information on anything and everything related to the subject of footwear.

Did you know that in our lifetime we will walk the equivalent of three and a half times around the earth?

F The Footwear Café

After your visit to the museum, you may like to pay a visit to our footwear café. Although the decor is probably not what you would expect to find in a museum, we hope you will enjoy our footwear-related art collection. Finally, you must try some of our speciality cakes – all with a footwear theme, of course!

C Now read the brochure again and answer the questions, choosing from paragraphs A-F.

Where would you

go if you were a shoe designer? *1*

see something which stopped people's feet from becoming too big? *2*

look at a singer's shoes? *3*

go to see paintings of shoes? *4*

find a light which looked like footwear? *5*

Which paragraph tells us about

footwear belonging to an astronaut? *6*

how far people walk? *7*

when people started to wear footwear? *8*

somewhere to relax in unusual surroundings? *9*

people who had to wear their employer's footwear? *10*

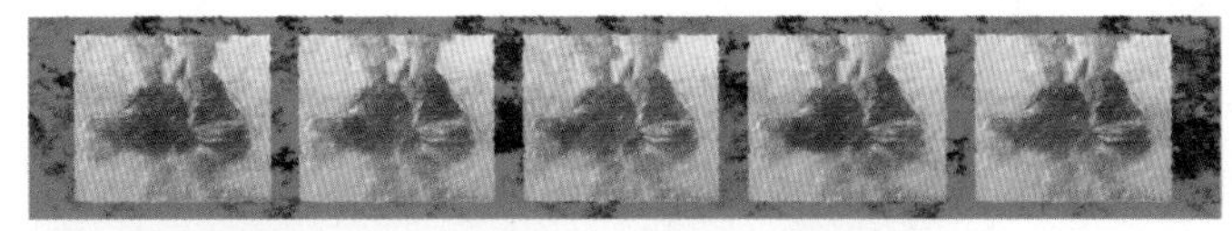

Vocabulary Link

D Underline the words or phrases in the brochure which mean:

1 things we see in a museum (A)

2 famous person (B)

3 whole (B)

4 very large (B)

5 tie tightly (C)

6 stop something happening (C)

7 hard, reddish-brown metal (D)

8 including everything (E)

E Complete the sentences with one of the colours shown and circle the whole phrase.

blue white black red green

1 Gill went as .... as a beetroot when the heel fell off her new boots.

2 Mum's fingers were .... with cold because she had lost her gloves.

3 Everybody was happy when we decided to have a .... wedding.

4 My teacher gave me a .... look when I wore my mini skirt to class.

5 I'm .... and .... all over after falling down the stairs.

6 Jane was .... with envy when she saw my new watch.

7 Out of the ...., David bought me a new dress.

8 The shoplifter was caught ....-handed when she tried to steal the gold earrings.

F Circle the word that completes the sentences correctly.

1 The assistant asked me what **number / size** shoes I wanted.

2 My brother is really strange – he wears trousers that make him **look like / look** a clown.

3 The model was **carrying / wearing** gold shoes, gold earrings and gold nail varnish.

4 My mother had a very slim **waste / waist** when she was younger – now she looks like a barrel!

5 The shoplifter tried to tell the manager that he had left the **receipt / recipe** at home.

6 'If the dress doesn't **fit / suit** your mother, we can exchange it for a larger size.'

7 The bride's veil **matched / suited** her dress perfectly.

8 Every afternoon, she **wears / puts** on her oldest clothes and does some work in the garden.

Grammar Link

Modals – Ability, Obligation and Necessity

*... you **can** see exhibits from all over the world.*
*You **can** find out about shoes, boots and sandals ...*

Which word in these examples is used to show the ability to do something in the present? ....

Which word do we use to show ability in the past?
....

What are the negative forms of these two words?
....

Remember

When it is not possible to use **can** or **could**, we use **be able to**. See Grammar Reference page 102.

Read these examples from the text.

*Finally, you **must** try some of our speciality cakes ...*

*... Napoleon Bonaparte's servants **had to** wear his shoes to break them in ...*

Which words in these two examples show a need to do something? ....

Which of the verbs in the sentences above is used to show the past? ....

What are the negative forms of **must** and **have to**?
....

Now read these two sentences.

*We **mustn't** leave early.*
*We **don't have to** leave early.*

Is there a difference in meaning between the negative forms of these verbs? ....

Complete the following rules.

.... is used when somebody tells us not to do something.

.... is used to show that an action is not necessary.

Study 4.1 of the Grammar Reference on page 102 before you do the task.

G Complete the following sentences by using **can**, **must** or **have to** in the correct form.

1 Mark .... walk until he was nearly two years old.

2 We .... bring our slippers because the airline gave us everything free.

3 I .... walk in high heels now but I never .... when I was a child.

4 You really .... work so hard!

5 They .... wait for a later train because there are no seats on this one.

6 You .... look at the new boots on sale in the market.

Listening Link

H Listen to models Zoe Lace and Lesley 'Legs Eleven' talking about their experiences during a recent fashion show. Tick (✓) the boxes to show whether the statements are **true** or **false**.

	T	F
1 Both models nearly fell over on the catwalk.		
2 Neither model wanted to wear the high-heeled boots.		
3 Zoe was the only one who had to dance for the TV cameras.		
4 'Legs Eleven' never has to diet.		

Speaking Link

I Work with a partner. Discuss this topic and the questions below. ***You can't judge a book by its cover.***

- What does this mean? Do you agree?
- How important are the clothes you wear?
- When is it important to think carefully about what you wear?
- When you meet people for the first time, are you influenced by their appearance?
- When do you worry about the clothes you wear?

Now report back to the class.

Grammar Link

although, despite/in spite of

Read this sentence from the brochure.

***Although** the decor is probably not what you would expect to find in a museum, we hope you will enjoy our footwear-related art collection.*

Now imagine a person who has visited the museum writing about it. This person could write:

***Despite/In spite of** the strange decor, the museum was fantastic.*

***Despite/In spite of** being strangely decorated, the museum was fantastic.*

Complete the following rules.

.... is used before a subject and verb.
.... is used before a noun or a verb in the gerund form.

J Complete the sentences by adding **although** or **despite/in spite of**.

1 .... her injury, she insisted on wearing heels.

2 .... they got up late, they managed to get to the fashion show on time.

3 .... the weather wasn't very good, the photographer took enough good pictures for the catalogue.

4 She modelled the swimwear .... having a cold.

5 .... being rather tired, Julie worked late.

Writing Link

K *Use your ideas from the Speaking Link to write a composition about the advantages and disadvantages of being fashion-conscious.*

Before you write your composition, look at the topic sentences opposite and the outline of the composition and decide which topic sentence is for each paragraph.

HINTS

In a composition, the reader should understand from the first sentence of each paragraph what that paragraph is about. This first sentence, which explains what the whole paragraph is about, is called a TOPIC SENTENCE.

a There are some people who believe that it is very important to be fashion-conscious.

b On the whole, there is something to be said for both points of view.

c The subject of fashion and whether or not it is important is not new.

d On the other hand, others feel that the clothes someone wears is not important at all.

Composition Outline

Paragraph 1 ☐
Introduce the general subject you are going to discuss. Say that there are two sides to the subject.

Paragraph 2 ☐
Discuss the advantages of the subject. Give examples or details to support your ideas.

Paragraph 3 ☐
Discuss the disadvantages of the subject. Give examples or details to support your ideas.

Paragraph 4 ☐
Give a balanced comment on the subject. You can also give your opinion here.

Helpful Expressions

There are people who think/believe (that) ...
Some people think/believe (that) ...
On the other hand, others feel/argue that ...
In addition, ...
Furthermore, ...
Moreover, ...
However, ...
On the whole, ...

advantages, benefits, pros, arguments in favour

disadvantages, drawbacks, cons, arguments against

L You are ready to write your composition, using the topic sentences and the outline from above. (80-100 words)

Review 1 

 Complete the following text by putting **one** word in each space.

HOPING TO BECOME FAMOUS

When I (1) ......was...... fifteen years old, I (2) .... play the guitar quite well so my friend and I started our own band. That was three years (3) .... Now, we (4) .... play much better. In fact, (5) .... we were playing at one of our high school dances, many people suggested we should send a tape of our music to a record company.

(6) .... it is very difficult to become real musicians, we are (7) .... to try. At the (8) ...., we are making a tape which we will send to three or four record companies as soon as it (9) .... ready. Then we will just (10) .... to wait and see what happens.

Nearly all our friends hope that we will be successful and they keep on asking us what we will do (11) .... we are famous. They seem to be certain we can make it, but we are not so sure, so we reply: 'Let's wait and see, (12) .... we?'

 Decide which phrase **a**, **b** or **c** completes the second sentence in each pair so that it has a similar meaning to the sentence before it.

1 Louise is an engineer, isn't she?
Louise works .... she?
- **a** as an engineer, isn't
- ⓑ as an engineer, doesn't
- **c** an engineer, doesn't

2 I'll finish my training and then I'll be able to work with my father.
I'll be able to work with my father when .... my training.
- **a** I finish
- **b** I will finish
- **c** I am finishing

3 Charlotte plans to decorate her flat next month.
Charlotte .... her flat next month.
- **a** will decorate
- **b** is going to decorate
- **c** decorates

4 They went to the concert despite being very tired.
They went to the concert although .... very tired.
- **a** that they were
- **b** being
- **c** they were

5 I spoke to Mr Farr during the tea break.
I spoke to Mr Farr .... a cup of tea.
- **a** while he was having
- **b** he was having
- **c** when he has

6 Cheryl always goes out on Saturday afternoon.
Cheryl .... at home on Saturday afternoon.
- **a** never is
- **b** is never
- **c** is always not

7 It was not necessary for him to wear formal clothes at the meeting.
He .... formal clothes at the meeting.
- **a** didn't have to wear
- **b** mustn't wear
- **c** couldn't wear

Use the words given in capitals at the end of each sentence to form a word that fits in the space.

1 You must try some cheesecake if you go to that café; it's their ....speciality.......... . **SPECIAL**
2 This track is .... ; there are no lyrics. **INSTRUMENT**
3 Don't climb up there, it's .... **DANGER**
4 I would like to live in a big, ... flat. **SPACE**
5 Oh, I've read that book; I thought it was .... **FASCINATE**
6 The .... should do something to help poor people. **GOVERN**
7 The fire fighter was awarded a medal for his .... **BRAVE**
8 I went to the new hotel on George Street last week. It's really ...., you know. **LUXURY**
9 He has stopped working as a fire fighter for .... reasons. **HEALTHY**
10 .... say that listening to very loud music can damage your hearing. **RESEARCH**

In each line of the paragraph below, there is one extra word. Circle the word that is not needed.

Richard's Story

1 Richard was a musician and he lived with his family in (always) very cramped conditions.
2 When he couldn't find work, he queued up at the soup kitchen for with his wife and two
3 children, so that they had a hot meal at least once a day. According to by his friend,
4 Bob, there was a way to find out 'work' very easily. When Bob explained what
5 to do, Richard thought: 'What's good for to him, is the same for me, too.' So, late
6 one night, Richard has climbed over the wall behind the big shop near his house. He
7 found a way in and saw that the shop had a rarely big selection of clothes. He took
8 everything that was in the fashion at the time and put it in his big bag. Just as he
9 was leaving, feeling proud of himself, he was arrested for by the police. The shop had
10 an alarm system that couldn't to be seen or heard by burglars – so Richard was caught red-handed!

A Have you ever been to places like the ones in the photographs? Would you like to go to any of the places in the photographs? Give reasons why or why not.

Reading Link

B Read the tourist guidebook quickly to find out where you would go in Sydney to see the whole city.

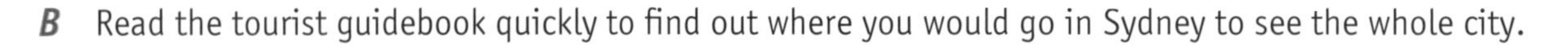

Welcome to Sydney!

1

It wasn't until 1788 that the first group of 736 convicts arrived at what is now known as Sydney Harbour, even though convicts of minor crimes had been transported from England to the colonies for a hundred years before that. As time passed their numbers grew and a new community took shape. The government stopped sending people when the Gold Rush of 1851 showed that the threat of going to Australia was actually encouraging crime instead of preventing it!

2

The city is dominated by the harbour, which people have described as one of the most spectacular in the world. There are three things which you must not – and indeed cannot – miss. Firstly, there is Sydney Harbour Bridge, one of the largest single-arch bridges in the world. Secondly, the Sydney Opera House is a landmark which most visitors anticipate with pleasure. Finally, don't miss Fort Denison, where prisoners were kept in solitary confinement for days on a diet of bread and water. The best way to get around is by boat or hydrofoil, both of which have regular services leaving from Circular Quay. If you prefer to do things at your own pace, why not hire one of the many boats available for this purpose?

3

Water plays a very big role in the inhabitants' leisure time. There are 27 miles of beaches to the north and south of Sydney, so it's hardly surprising that the locals spend so much time in the water! Two of the best-known beaches are Manly Beach and Bondi Beach, where the 'beautiful young people' of Sydney have been showing off their skills ever since surfing carnivals were first organised there.

4

For those tourists who would also like to see somewhere other than Sydney, the Blue Mountains are well worth a visit. They get their name from the fact that when you look at them from a distance, they are covered in a blue mist which comes from the small drops of eucalyptus oil in the air. Wentworth Falls and the view from the Scenic Skyway (a cable car high in the sky) are both breathtaking.

5

However, if you don't have the time – or the desire – to leave Sydney, don't worry; there's plenty to do in the city. For the best view of Sydney, visit Centre Point Tower. High above the city you can dine in the revolving restaurant, and no sea-food lover should leave Sydney without trying our world-famous Sydney Rock Oysters. For the night-owls among you, make sure you go to Oxford Street and King's Cross to check out the city's nightlife.

If you have never been to Sydney before, pack your bags right away! We are sure you will enjoy yourselves and have a very pleasant stay in our city.

C Now read the tourist guidebook again and choose which sentence best summarises paragraphs 1-5.

- *A* See the best of Sydney's sights by sea. ☐
- *B* The people of Sydney like getting their feet wet! ☐
- *C* You'll enjoy eating and drinking in Sydney. ☐
- *D* The first residents of Sydney were criminals. ☐
- *E* There is spectacular scenery just outside Sydney. ☐

Vocabulary Link

D Complete the sentences with words from the tourist guidebook. (**HINT**: they are all people!)

1. The .... of the island rely on tourism to survive.
2. He's a ....; he never goes to bed before midnight!
3. There was a warning on TV that the .... who escaped from prison last night are armed and dangerous.
4. .... are only allowed in the temple at certain times of the day.
5. We had a great holiday in Greece; the .... were really friendly.
6. I really hate this city in the summer; there are .... everywhere!

E Match these words from paragraph 2 with their meanings.

Words	Meanings
1 spectacular	a alone
2 landmark	b ready for use
3 anticipate	c something which is easily seen and recognised from far away
4 solitary	d very impressive
5 confinement	e expect, look forward to
6 available	f imprisonment

F Write in the correct prefix **dis-**, **ir-** or **un-** to change these words from the tourist guidebook. (You will have to make a small change to one of the words!) Then tick the words that have become negative.

1 .... available	6 .... organised
2 .... covered	7 .... pleasant
3 .... encouraging	8 .... pleasure
4 .... known	9 .... regular
5 .... like	10 .... surprising

Grammar Link

Past Simple, Present Perfect Simple, Present Perfect Continuous

Which tense is used below? ....

It ***wasn't*** *until 1788 that the first group of 736 convicts* ***arrived*** *...*

Why is this tense used? ....

....

Which tense is used below? ....

....

... the harbour, which people ***have described*** *as one of the most spectacular...*

Why is this tense used? ....

....

Which tense is used below? ....

... the 'beautiful young people' of Sydney ***have been showing off*** *their skills ever since ...*

Why is this tense used? ....

....

Complete the following rules.

The .... tense is used to talk about completed actions or states when the time is not mentioned or is not important.

The .... tense is used to talk about how long something has been in progress.

Study 5.1 and 5.2 of the Grammar Reference on page 103 before you do the task.

G Put the verb in brackets into the Past Simple, the Present Perfect Simple or the Present Perfect Continuous form.

1. The last time they .... (swim) at Bondi beach was in 1993.
2. She .... (write) tourist guidebooks for five years now.
3. Jack .... (win) the surfing championships three times.
4. I .... (go) to the museum last Monday.
5. I .... (read) all of the guidebooks, so I'm ready to go on a tour of the city.
6. How long .... (Tom / work) as a tour guide?
7. Sharon .... (eat) snake meat so she knows what it tastes like.

Listening Link

H Listen to some people talking in different places. Listen for the main point of each part and choose the best answer **a**, **b** or **c**.

1 You overhear two men talking in a seven-star hotel in Dubai. What are they discussing?
   a the size of the building
   b the cost of the food
   c the gold leaf on the floor

2 Listen to this woman speaking. What does she want to do?
   a visit the offices of the United Nations
   b take a photograph of a Gothic building
   c take a course at the University of Geneva

3 A man in a travel agent's is talking to a customer on the phone. What is he explaining to the customer?
   a how to get to the island of Zakynthos
   b the history of the island of Zante
   c what the weather is like on the island

4 You hear two girls talking on the school bus. What are they talking about?
   a There was a problem with question 5 in the geography exam.
   b They couldn't remember the seven provinces of Kenya.
   c Neither of them could remember what Kenya's main products were.

5 You hear these two friends talking in the library. What are they doing?
   a researching into place names
   b doing their geography homework
   c entering a competition

Grammar Link

have been to, have gone to

Compare these two sentences.

If you ***have*** *never* ***been to*** *Sydney before, pack your bags right away!*

She can't play squash this week because she ***has gone to*** *Sydney on business.*

Which of these two sentences talks about a person who is in Sydney now, or on the way there? ....
....

Correct the following sentence.

I've gone to Sweden and I can tell you that it gets very cold there in winter.

Complete the following rules.

.... is used when a person has visited a place and has come back.
.... is used when a person is visiting a place and hasn't come back yet.

I Complete the sentences with **have/has been** or **have/has gone**.

1 John will be able to tell you about Japan because he .... there.

2 She .... to Spain but she'll be back next week.

3 They .... to the Fiji Islands twice and they say it's great for a holiday.

4 Karen and Lucy .... to the museum so we'll see them later.

for and since

... where the 'beautiful young people' of Sydney have been showing off their skills ever ***since*** *surf carnivals were first organised there.*

... this prisoner has been kept in solitary confinement ***for*** *days ...*

Complete the rules.

Since and **for** can be used to talk about how long an action has been in progress or how long a state has existed until now. .... is followed by a specific point in time and .... is followed by a period of time.

J Complete the following sentences by adding **for** or **since**.

1 I have been trying to contact Ian .... I arrived in town.

2 We have been waiting for a bus .... at least half an hour.

3 We've been having trouble with our travel agent .... December.

4 She's known him .... they met on the beach in Spain.

5 They've been using that airline .... a number of years.

Speaking Link

K Ask and answer these questions with a partner, using the expressions to help you. Don't forget to give reasons for your answers.

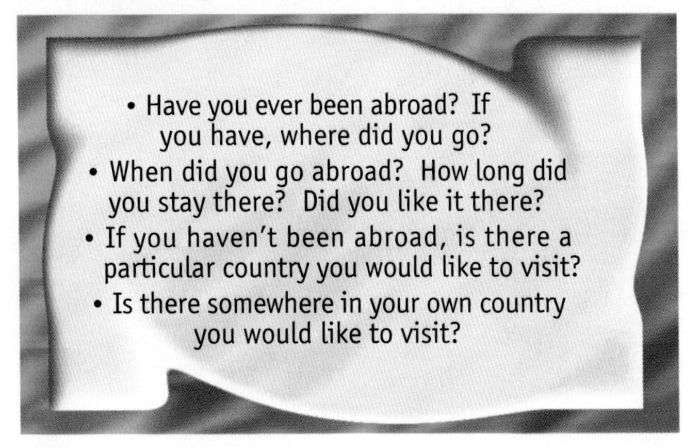

- Have you ever been abroad? If you have, where did you go?
- When did you go abroad? How long did you stay there? Did you like it there?
- If you haven't been abroad, is there a particular country you would like to visit?
- Is there somewhere in your own country you would like to visit?

I've been to ...
I've never been abroad.
I went to ... (in 1999 / last summer / three years ago).
I stayed there for (two weeks / a month).
I really liked ... because ... .
I would like to go to ... because ... .

L Read the story below which describes a strange experience on holiday and then fill the gaps with the most suitable word or phrase from the box.

a	until	**d**	then
b	when	**e**	eventually/at last
c	suddenly/all of a sudden		

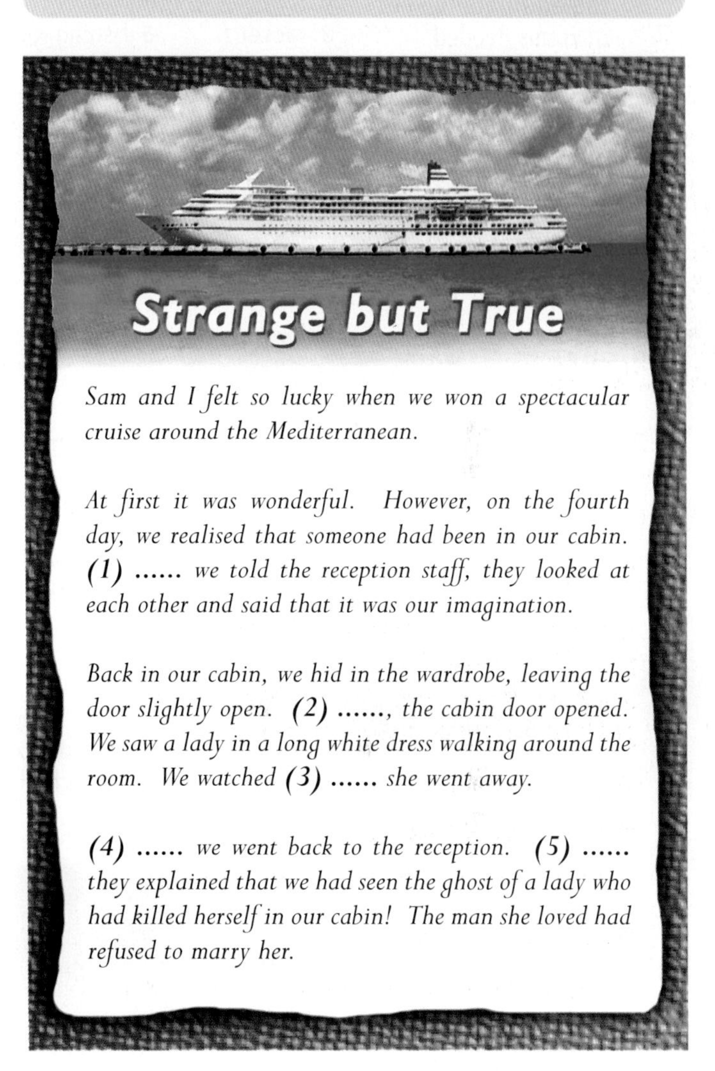

Strange but True

Sam and I felt so lucky when we won a spectacular cruise around the Mediterranean.

At first it was wonderful. However, on the fourth day, we realised that someone had been in our cabin. (1) ...... we told the reception staff, they looked at each other and said that it was our imagination.

Back in our cabin, we hid in the wardrobe, leaving the door slightly open. (2) ......, the cabin door opened. We saw a lady in a long white dress walking around the room. We watched (3) ...... she went away.

(4) ...... we went back to the reception. (5) ...... they explained that we had seen the ghost of a lady who had killed herself in our cabin! The man she loved had refused to marry her.

Writing Link

HINTS

To write a good story you should think about five things:

1. *Ideas*
   Keep them simple.
2. *Tenses*
   Use the correct tenses.
3. *Linking words*
   Use appropriate linking words.
4. *Vocabulary*
   Using a wide range of vocabulary makes your story more interesting.
5. *Paragraphs*
   A story with paragraphs in a logical order can make a story much more exciting.

M *Read the hints opposite, and then write your own story entitled* ***Strange but True.***

Remember to use some of the words and phrases from task L above. (100-120 words)

Story Outline

Paragraph 1	Think about these question words to start your story: Who? When? Where? Why?
Paragraph 2	Continue your story up to the crisis point (climax).
Paragraph 3	Describe the climax.
Paragraph 4	Say what happened as a result of the event.

Unit 6 Sports and Hobbies

A Match the sports and hobbies in the photos with the equipment or items needed to practise them.

1 film
2 club
3 racket
4 ramp
5 trainers
6 fishing rod

B Read through the article and explain what Zorbing is.

The Zorb

New Zealand has already given us lots of excitement with bungee jumping. Now, it's the turn of the Zorb!

Have you ever wondered what it would be like to roll down a hill at speeds of up to 48 kph inside a huge ball? Perhaps not, but that was the thought Andrew Akers had while he was looking through some drawings by Leonardo da Vinci, or so he says. Wherever the idea came from, Andrew and ex-research scientist Dwane van der Sluis began designing such a ball, which they called a Zorb.

The job was far from easy. 'We took the prototype to our bank manager, hoping to get a loan, but he wasn't very enthusiastic,' says Andrew. 'His actual words were: "That's a nice beach ball," which didn't really give us much confidence.' Luckily, they were not discouraged and each one decided to design a sphere separately. 'Dwane's sphere was too small and mine was too large. Each one was useless on its own, but we put one inside the other and the Zorb was born.'

The Zorbonaut, the person enjoying the thrill of Zorbing, climbs into the inside ball through a hole or kind of tunnel which passes through the outside ball. There is 70 cm of air

between the Zorbonaut and the ground so the person is protected from the effects of the ball bouncing along. Now the Zorb has been fully tested to make sure it is completely safe, which wasn't what happened originally. 'I broke my arm in the prototype, but we have done our best to prevent injury since then,' says Andrew.

Only the strongest materials have been used to make Zorbs. The plastic does not tear and the outside ball is designed so that it does not lose its shape. After designers had been experimenting for a long time, they made Zorbs with harnesses to keep people safely in position while they are Zorbing on their own or with a friend.

Zorbing is so new that Andrew and Dwane still have to answer questions about it. 'People asked us a lot of questions at first, but we were able to answer them because we had thought about the problems carefully before the Zorb went on sale,' says Dwane. 'And one thing they still want to know is whether they will be sick in it. Well, we've had over 10,000 Zorbonauts and not one has been sick yet!'

So, what's it like? 'It's not like being in a tumble dryer and it doesn't turn your stomach, but the feeling is very very strange. Why don't you try it?' says Andrew, encouragingly.

C Read the article carefully and choose the best answer **a**, **b**, **c** or **d** for each of the questions (1-5).

1 How did Andrew and Dwane feel after their meeting with the bank manager?

a happy
b confident
c disappointed
d jealous

2 Whose design did they use to make the original Zorb?

a Dwane's and Andrew's
b Dwane's
c Andrew's
d A design engineer's

3 Why doesn't a Zorbonaut get hurt when the Zorb bounces?

a There is a hole in the Zorb.
b There is protection from a layer of air.
c The Zorb is made of a soft material.
d The Zorbonaut wears a special suit.

4 What have Andrew and Dwane concentrated on most?

a making the Zorb bounce higher
b making the Zorb lighter
c making a Zorb for two people
d making the Zorb safe

5 How does Andrew describe Zorbing?

a It makes your stomach feel funny.
b It is a very unusual experience.
c It is like floating in space.
d It is like a ride at the funfair.

D The words and phrases below have been taken from the article. Choose the word or phrase closest in meaning to each one.

1 separately (para 3)	a quickly b not together
2 thrill (para 4)	a danger b excitement
3 effects (para 4)	a results b injuries
4 bouncing (para 4)	a flying in a straight line b springing up and down
5 tear (para 5)	a break open b pull
6 harnesses (para 5)	a special shoes b straps that hold someone in place

E Match the phrasal verbs with the explanations.

1 go on	a cause to fall
2 knock down	b chase
3 run after	c escape
4 run away	d happen

Now put the phrasal verbs into the sentences in their correct form.

1 The horse .... the fence and then threw its rider, too.

2 Four young athletes .... from the Spartans' Junior Training Camp in the last year.

3 I wondered what .... when I saw my friend rolling down the hill inside a strange ball.

4 The dog .... the ball when the golfer hit it too far away from the green.

F Circle the word that completes the sentences correctly.

1 The **umpire / referee** stopped the exciting tennis match when it started to rain heavily.

2 People who **look at / watch** a rugby match are called spectators.

3 Fran wore the latest design in **ski / sky** boots during the slalom.

4 You can see the ball more clearly when you watch the **game / play** on TV.

5 Do you know who **won / beat** the football World Cup in 1994?

6 The final **score / mark** was 4-2.

Grammar Link

Past Simple, Past Perfect Simple, Past Perfect Continuous

Look at the tenses used in this example.

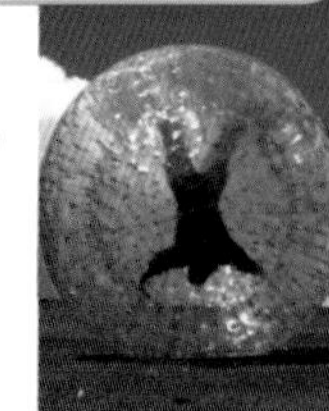

*People **asked** us a lot of questions at first, but we **were able to answer** them because we **had thought** about the problems carefully before the Zorb **went** on sale.*

Which of the verbs talks about an action which happened before the others? ....
Which tense is this verb in? ....

Which tense is used together with the Past Simple in the following example? ....

*After designers **had been experimenting** for a long time, they made Zorbs with harnesses ...*

Why is this tense used? ....
....

Complete the following rules.

The .... tense is used to talk about an action which happened or a state which existed .... another event, state or time in the past. The .... tense is used to talk about actions which were in progress until a certain time in the past.

Study the Grammar Reference on page 103 before you do the task.

G Put the verbs in brackets into the Past Simple, Past Perfect Simple or Past Perfect Continuous forms.

1 I .... (know) about the accident because Norman .... (tell) me about it earlier in the afternoon.

2 Nobody .... (beat) the Russian wrestler before the last Olympic Games.

3 My uncle .... (collect) stamps for many years before I .... (start).

4 Tina .... (not be able) to answer the questions since she .... (not read) the book.

5 Robert .... (feel) better after the doctor .... (give) him some medicine.

6 Max .... (be) frightened because he .... (never do) a bungee jump before.

Listening Link

H Listen to a sports announcement at the Olympic Games. For questions 1-4, complete the notes which tell us what instructions the speaker is giving to visiting athletes. You may write a word or a short phrase in each box.

Athletes must (1) __________ from the Olympic doctor before going onto the track.

Athletes are advised to warm up properly to relax and prevent (2) __________

Occupants of rooms in the Olympic Village can (3) __________

The new sports bags are made of (4) __________ that is easily washed.

Speaking Link

I These are photographs of people doing different hobbies. Look at the photographs and compare and contrast them, saying what type of person you think would be interested in taking up hobbies like these.

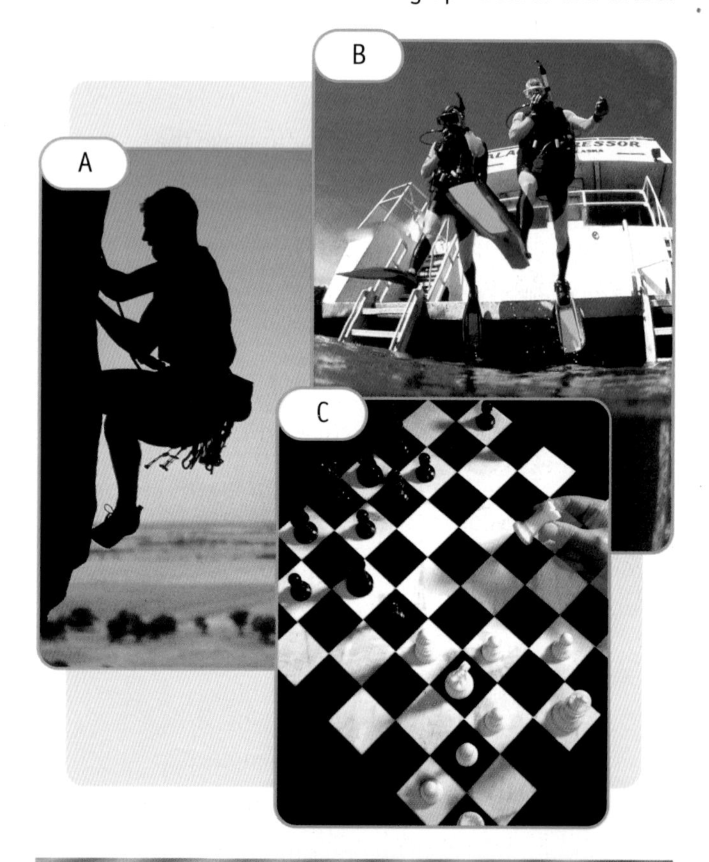

- Have you ever tried any of these activities?
- Would you like to do any of these hobbies in your free time?
- What are your hobbies?

J *You have seen the following advertisement in the local newspaper and have made some notes. Write a letter asking for further information about the points you have made.*

Have you decided to take the plunge?

Are you one of those people who has always wanted to learn how to scuba dive, but has never had the time? If so, don't miss the Extreme Sports Centre's summer school at Golden Beach Bay.

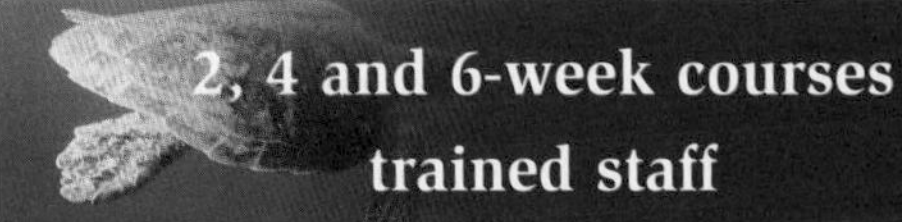

2, 4 and 6-week courses
trained staff

BOOK NOW TO AVOID DISAPPOINTMENT!

Extreme Sports Centre, Golden Beach Bay, West Rock, 10632, Coraltown

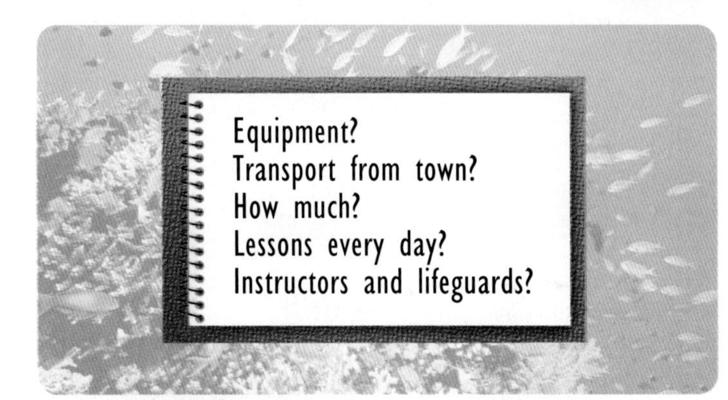

When you write a formal letter asking for information, you must remember to be polite. One way to do this is to use indirect questions.

Direct question

How many students are there in a class?

This sounds rather too direct and perhaps even rude.

Indirect question

I would like to know how many students there are in a class.

This sounds much more polite. Notice how the word order has changed.

Other ways to ask indirect questions

Could you let me know ...?
Could you tell me ...?
I wonder if you could let me know ...
I wonder if you could tell me ...

K Use the phrases to change these direct questions into indirect questions. There is more than one possible answer

1 Do you supply students with all the necessary equipment?

....

....

2 Is there any transport from town?

....

....

3 How much do the courses cost?

....

....

4 Are there lessons every day?

....

....

5 Are there instructors and lifeguards?

....

....

L Now write your letter, using the indirect sentences from task K and the letter outline below. Try to organise your points into logical paragraphs. (100-120 words)

Letter Outline

Greeting	Dear Sir/Madam
Paragraph 1	Say where and when you saw the advertisement. Say that you would like some more information
Paragraph 2	Ask about the courses/lessons.
Paragraph 3	Ask about equipment/ instructors/transport from town.
Closing paragraph	Say that you would be grateful if they gave you the information you have requested. Say that you are looking forward to their reply.
Signing off	Yours faithfully (your name)

A Some people say that when the weather changes, people change their mood. Using the words given, say how weather conditions can make people feel.

MOODS	WEATHER CONDITIONS
1 bored	gale force winds a
2 depressed	bright sunshine b
3 excited	rain c
4 restless	thunderstorm d
5 nervous	snowstorm e
6 cheerful	fog f

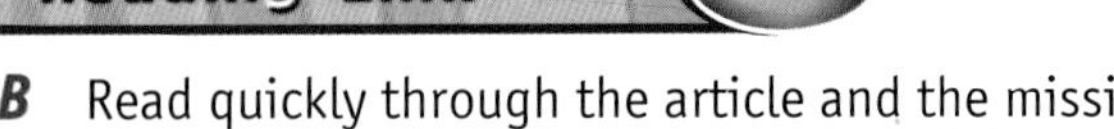

B Read quickly through the article and the missing paragraphs to find out what effect a cloudy sky at night will have on the following day's temperature.

Weather Forecasting

Today is 13th July and it is snowing in London. In Athens, they are having the driest summer for many years. Temperatures have risen to over 41ºC and the beaches have been crowded since 8 o'clock this morning. On the other side of the world, people in parts of Australia are experiencing the worst floods for a century.

1

In a rather small building in the centre of the city, Tony was surprised to find an army of weather scientists with their computerised charts, carefully studying the latest 'surprises'. The telephone rang constantly as members of the public phoned in for advice about the weather, double-checking forecasts they had heard on the news that day.

2

It is not only scientists who look at unusual signs. Ross Lindy, who has been working in the Met Office for over 15 years, said: 'My mother used to say that it was going to rain every time the cows lay down in the fields, and she was always right!' Many old people have their own 'methods' of predicting the weather but nowadays things are more scientific. In fact, it is surprising how even a schoolchild can make day-to-day predictions with just a little bit of information. So how is the weather actually forecast?

3

If you want a more scientific approach, then you need to do your physics homework. We know that the earth is heated by the sun during the day. If skies are clear and blue, then more heat reaches the earth's surface. As a result, temperatures will be higher.

4

However, if you are a more advanced forecaster, you can check the weather map to see where there is a cold front. If the atmosphere is also very humid, then you may see rain. The weather map will also tell you where there are high or low pressure centres. None of these methods needs special knowledge or technology.

5

Unfortunately, improved technology was not much help in predicting some of the natural disasters that have happened in the last decades, like the torrential rains at the end of 1999 that caused floods, killing thousands in Venezuela.

C Five paragraphs were removed from the article you have just read. See if you can put them back in their correct place.

HINTS

Read the text carefully looking for words and phrases before and after each gap which link the missing paragraphs to the text.

A
For the beginner, the simplest method is to think that the forecast conditions will continue to be the same. Therefore, if it is freezing cold today, then it is likely to be the same tomorrow. This method only works well where weather conditions are usually stable. In addition, it is quite accurate for predicting long-range weather conditions.

B
It is a different matter for the professional forecaster, whose weather predictions are carried out using computers and complex programs. The computer can predict temperature, pressure, wind and rainfall. Then the weather forecaster can examine how the day's weather will be affected. This method is accurate, but it is not recommended for the beginner.

C
On the other hand, if there are clouds in the sky, these will reflect the sun's rays and this will lower the temperature. At night, the opposite happens. These are conclusions that can be reached with just a little common sense.

D
What has happened to our weather and why can't weather forecasters be more accurate? Tony Sleet took a trip to the local Meteorological Office to find out what is going on.

E
In addition to these daily forecasts, weather scientists are also responsible for long-range forecasts and for 'spotting' anything unusual that might appear in the sky.

Vocabulary Link

D Circle the two words in these groups that are linked to the headings of each box.

Weather	Nature
approach	information
recommend	scientist
conditions	field
thunderstorm	disaster
surface	landing

Flood	Forecast
atmosphere	prediction
rain	century
pressure	humid
water	advice
physics	weather

Computer	Temperature
scientific	rise
program	Athens
long-range	crowded
screen	freezing
daily	complex

E Complete the sentences with a form of the word in capitals. All the words are in the article.

1 The .... place in the world is the Atacama Desert in Chile. ***DRY***

2 The desert is about 1,000 km .... and it runs from Argentina in the east to the Pacific beaches in the west. ***LENGTH***

3 Rain has never been recorded in some .... stations in the area. ***METEOROLOGY***

4 .... rains have fallen three times each century. ***TORRENT***

5 Nothing has .... in this desert for years. ***GROW***

6 It is .... how fog and cloud often appear over the desert, but disappear again without any sign of rain. ***SURPRISE***

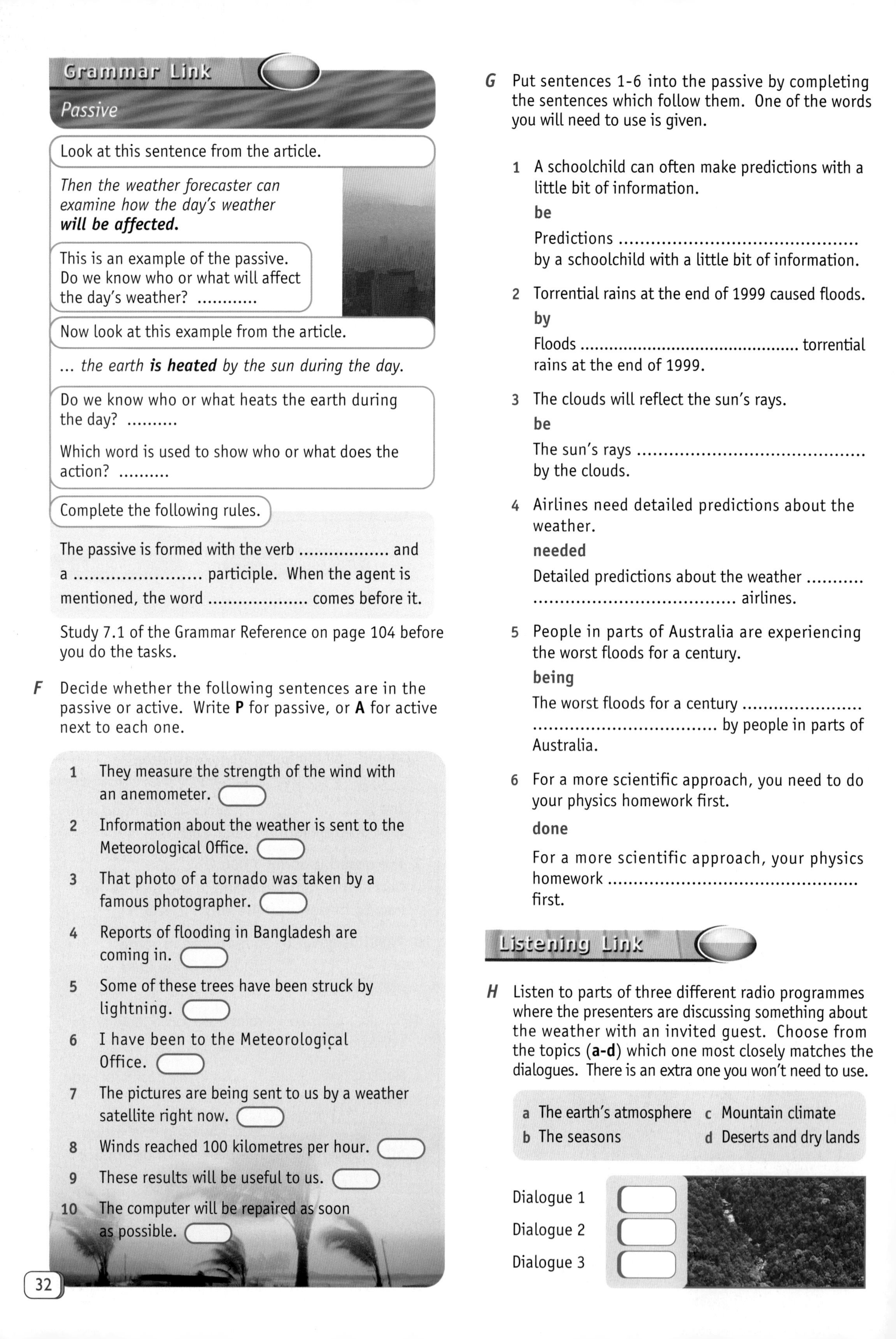

Grammar Link

Passive

Look at this sentence from the article.

Then the weather forecaster can examine how the day's weather ***will be affected.***

This is an example of the passive. Do we know who or what will affect the day's weather? ....

Now look at this example from the article.

... the earth ***is heated*** *by the sun during the day.*

Do we know who or what heats the earth during the day? ....

Which word is used to show who or what does the action? ....

Complete the following rules.

The passive is formed with the verb .... and a .... participle. When the agent is mentioned, the word .... comes before it.

Study 7.1 of the Grammar Reference on page 104 before you do the tasks.

F Decide whether the following sentences are in the passive or active. Write **P** for passive, or **A** for active next to each one.

1 They measure the strength of the wind with an anemometer. ( )
2 Information about the weather is sent to the Meteorological Office. ( )
3 That photo of a tornado was taken by a famous photographer. ( )
4 Reports of flooding in Bangladesh are coming in. ( )
5 Some of these trees have been struck by lightning. ( )
6 I have been to the Meteorological Office. ( )
7 The pictures are being sent to us by a weather satellite right now. ( )
8 Winds reached 100 kilometres per hour. ( )
9 These results will be useful to us. ( )
10 The computer will be repaired as soon as possible. ( )

G Put sentences 1-6 into the passive by completing the sentences which follow them. One of the words you will need to use is given.

1 A schoolchild can often make predictions with a little bit of information.
be
Predictions .... by a schoolchild with a little bit of information.

2 Torrential rains at the end of 1999 caused floods.
by
Floods .... torrential rains at the end of 1999.

3 The clouds will reflect the sun's rays.
be
The sun's rays .... by the clouds.

4 Airlines need detailed predictions about the weather.
needed
Detailed predictions about the weather .... airlines.

5 People in parts of Australia are experiencing the worst floods for a century.
being
The worst floods for a century .... by people in parts of Australia.

6 For a more scientific approach, you need to do your physics homework first.
done
For a more scientific approach, your physics homework .... first.

Listening Link

H Listen to parts of three different radio programmes where the presenters are discussing something about the weather with an invited guest. Choose from the topics (**a-d**) which one most closely matches the dialogues. There is an extra one you won't need to use.

a The earth's atmosphere
b The seasons
c Mountain climate
d Deserts and dry lands

Dialogue 1 ( )
Dialogue 2 ( )
Dialogue 3 ( )

Speaking Link 

I Imagine that there has been a flood warning, and you must make sure that you have everything you need in your house. Working with a partner, put these items in order with the most important thing first. Use the expressions below to help you as well as the ones you learnt in Unit 3

matches | candles | tins of food | battery-operated radio | mobile phone

I think/believe (that) ... is the most important because ... .
I think we should choose ... because ... .
What do you think?
I agree to a certain extent, but ... .
Actually, I think ... is more important than ... because ... .

Now report back to the class.
Did anybody have the same ideas as you?

Grammar Link 

Adjectives ending in ***-ing*** *or* ***-ed***

Read these sentences from the article.

... it is ***surprising*** *how even a schoolchild can make day-to-day predictions ...*

... Tony was ***surprised*** *to find an army of weather scientists ...*

Which sentence contains an adjective which describes how somebody feels? ....

Which sentence contains an adjective which describes a situation? ....

Complete the following rule.

Adjectives which end in .... describe how somebody feels while adjectives which end in .... describe a thing, situation, place or person.

J Complete the sentences by using the words in capitals to form adjectives ending in **-ed** or **-ing**.

1 I got .... during the documentary on weather forecasting because it just wasn't .... ***BORE, INTEREST***

2 It was an .... storm, with trees and plants blowing everywhere. ***AMAZE***

3 She's the most .... person I've ever met. ***FASCINATE***

4 Why do you look so .... to see me doing my physics homework? ***SURPRISE***

5 The film was really .... ***EXCITE***

Writing Link 

We have already looked at writing a discursive composition in Unit 4. In this unit, we will look at how to write a discursive composition where you give your opinion about something. In this type of question, you have to decide which opinion you agree with before you start writing.

K Look at the question and the model, and complete the outline.

Some people believe that the weather can change our mood, while others think that the way we feel has nothing to do with the weather. Write a composition, giving your opinion on the subject.

The effect that the weather can have on our mood is something that causes disagreement. I believe that it can affect how we feel.

In Scandinavian countries, for example, it is a well-known fact that the lack of sunshine in winter can cause depression. There are even special 'light boxes' where you can go to feel better.

Another example of how the weather can affect your mood is the way you feel on a nice, sunny day. Seeing the sun makes you want to go out and have fun.

I believe that the weather can make a big difference to the way you feel. Wouldn't it be great to have sunshine all the time?

Composition Outline

Paragraph 1	Introduce the subject. Say that people have different opinions about this subject. Give your opinion.
Paragraphs 2 and 3	....
Paragraph 4	....

L Before writing a composition giving YOUR opinion on the subject, read the hint below. (100-120 words)

HINTS

Always try to justify the things you write. The reader will be more likely to believe what you have written if you justify yourself. To do this, you should explain what you mean and give examples.

A Discuss with a friend what you expect the people in the list think about the problem of litter.

- a student in secondary school
- a member of *Clean up Greece*
- a journalist
- the manager of a chocolate factory

What is YOUR opinion on the problem?

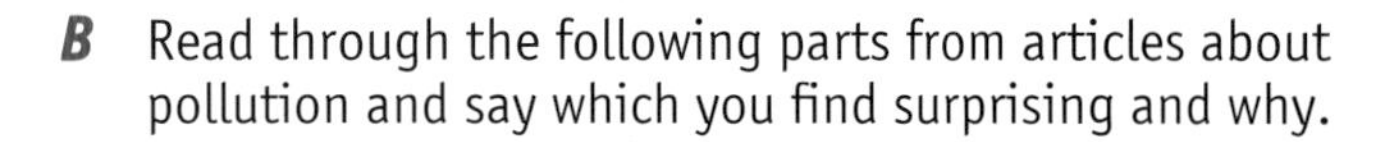

B Read through the following parts from articles about pollution and say which you find surprising and why.

THE WORLD IN DANGER

A Polluted Air

How would you like to wake up to the smell of bad eggs? Rumiya Dzhenblatova's family lives in southern Russia, near the largest chemical factory in the world. In Rumiya's living room there are five large round yellow balls hanging on the wall. Inside each ball there is a gas mask. 'When I see Luisa's nose bleeding, I know it's the gas again. If we are too slow to put on the masks, we feel sick,' says Rumiya.

B Polluted Seas

All our seas and oceans are polluted, but the Barents and Kara Seas, south of the Arctic Ocean, are more polluted than all the others. It is amazing how much waste has been dumped there. It is known that 14 nuclear reactors (four with fuel), one nuclear submarine with fuel and thousands of barrels of chemicals have been sunk there. It is not certain what this has done to the environment, but Norwegian scientists believe that in some places there is enough radioactive material in the Arctic food chain to destroy whole families of sea life.

C Polluted Earth

When certain gases mix with water in the atmosphere, they become acid rain. This can kill forests hundreds of miles away from the factories which make the gases. Then nothing can grow in the soil.

Apart from acid rain, the earth is also polluted by the chemicals that come from some old factories. Lead is one of the very dangerous metals that often gets into the soil and into the vegetables we eat. When these vegetables are eaten, the lead in them stays in the body and is particularly dangerous for children.

D Saving the World

Just saying you are shocked by pollution is not enough. Everyone must do something to protect the environment.

Clean up the World is an organisation which works with the United Nations. It has groups in many countries, including Greece. *Clean up Greece* has got an office in Athens and has been working to save the environment since 1993. Through education, *Clean up Greece* tells companies, the government and the public (especially young people) about the different ways to protect the environment. The idea is that today's school children, who will become tomorrow's decision-makers, will know what to do to prevent the destruction of our surroundings.

E Making a Difference

You may think that what you do will not be helpful enough because you can't do much, but you are wrong. If everyone is careful about what they throw away, there will be fewer rubbish dumps and the environment will benefit.

We should use the R theory, which stands for reduce, reuse, recycle and refuse. Firstly, reduce means having less rubbish than usual by eating snacks like bananas and oranges which are not in packets. Secondly, reuse means using plastic bags and bottles again, possibly to keep things in. Thirdly, recycle means using old things to make new ones and using certain vegetables to improve the soil in our gardens. Finally, refuse means not using products that are harmful to the environment.

Remember to help.

Some of this information was supplied by *Clean up Greece*
www.cleanupgreece.org.gr

C Read A-E again and answer the questions below.

Which part(s)

mentions food that is dangerous to eat? 1 ☐

mention places that are heavily polluted? 2 ☐ 3 ☐

Which part

talks about planning for the future? 4 ☐

mentions equipment that is used in emergencies? 5 ☐

mentions the importance of passing on information? 6 ☐

gives advice? 7 ☐

suggests that pollution in one area can affect other areas? 8 ☐

would be most likely to have an address you could write to? 9 ☐

10 Where is part E most probably taken from?

a a science book
b an information leaflet
c an advertisement
d a catalogue

Vocabulary Link

D The words and phrases below have been taken from parts A-E. Circle the word or phrase closest in meaning to each one.

1 polluted (part A)	a	made dirty
	b	changed
2 mask (part A)	a	something that hides the truth
	b	covering for part of the face
3 waste (part B)	a	part of your body
	b	something not needed any more
4 soil (part C)	a	earth
	b	make dirty
5 prevent (part D)	a	stop
	b	understand
6 benefit (part E)	a	be helped
	b	be understood

E Match the words to form phrases. Use a dictionary to find the meaning of any unknown words.

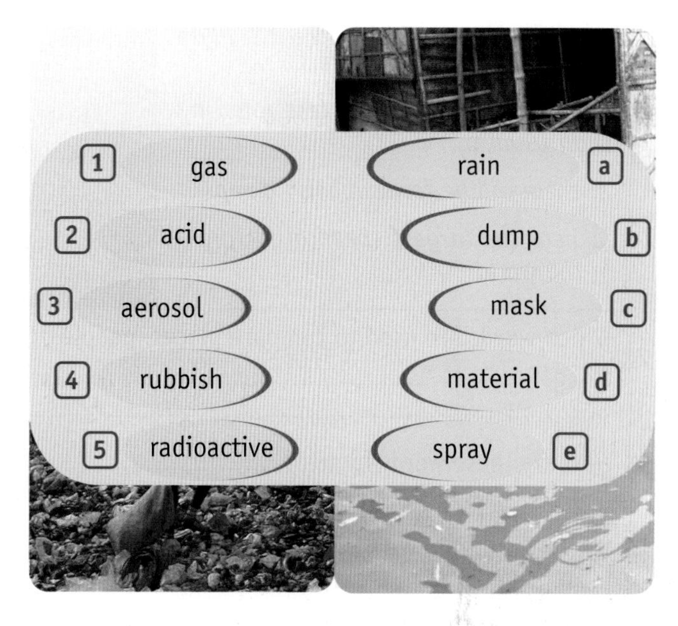

F Look at the examples from the text with **enough**, **too** and **very**.

*... there is **enough** radioactive material in the Arctic food chain to destroy whole families of sea life.*

*You may think that what you do will not be helpful **enough** ...*

*If we are **too** slow to put on the masks, we feel sick.*

*Lead is one of the **very** dangerous metals that often gets into the soil ...*

Now complete the following sentences by filling in the gaps with **enough**, **too** or **very** and putting the verbs into the correct form.

1 The river is .... polluted for animals and fish .... (live) in.

2 I don't think we are working quickly .... (save) our planet.

3 Will we have .... oxygen .... (breathe) in the future?

4 Some chemicals used in factories are .... dangerous indeed.

5 There aren't .... people helping the environment.

Grammar Link

Comparatives and Superlatives

Read these examples from the text.

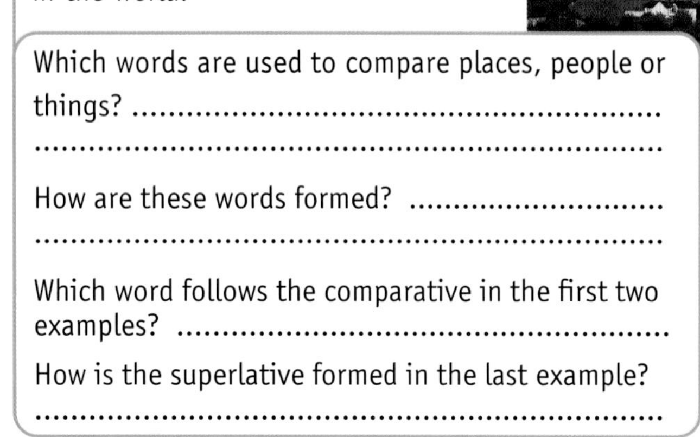

... south of the Arctic Ocean, are ***more*** *polluted* ***than*** *all the others.*

... reduce means having ***less*** *rubbish* ***than*** *usual ...*

... there will be ***fewer*** *rubbish dumps ...*

... near ***the largest*** *chemical factory in the world.*

Which words are used to compare places, people or things? ....

....

How are these words formed? ....

....

Which word follows the comparative in the first two examples? ....

How is the superlative formed in the last example?

....

See 8.2 of the Grammar Reference on page 105 for notes on spelling rules and irregular comparatives and superlatives before you do the task.

G Put the adjectives given into the comparative or superlative forms and add any other words necessary.

1 I don't know anyone .... (lazy) .... your brother! He never picks up the sweet papers from his bedroom floor.

2 The streets here are .... (dirty) ones I have ever seen.

3 Yvonne doesn't mind the summers in Greece because she has lived in .... (hot) countries.

4 Their country house was .... (far) away .... I thought, so the journey took .... (long).

5 .... (late) news from the North Sea is that the oil tanker crew were able to prevent oil from going into the sea.

6 People are .... (satisfied) with this report on oil pollution because it is .... (good) .... the last one the government wrote.

Adjectives: Word Order

How many adjectives describe the five balls in Rumiya's living room in this sentence? ....

In Rumiya's living room there are five ***large round yellow*** *balls hanging on the wall.*

When two or more adjectives are used together, they usually come in a set order. The most normal order is shown in the table below.

H Complete the table by giving two examples of each type of adjective.

opinion	size	age	shape	colour	nationality	material	NOUN
beautiful	*big*	*old*	*round*	*red*	*Chinese*	*cotton*	

I Read the following sentences. Put a tick (✓) against those which are correct, and correct those which are wrong.

1 I have recycled the beautiful white silk socks you bought ten years ago. ....

2 The *Clean Up* team found a small old porcelain vase on the beach ....

3 When the electricity was cut off, my aunt got out two new nice silver candlesticks. ....

4 The lovely little Swiss mountain was covered in rubbish dropped by tourists. ....

5 There was a white wooden square board showing the way to the lake. ....

Listening Link 

J Listen to Ninetta Hobbes talking about cleaning up beaches with the help of school children. Tick (✓) the boxes to show whether the answers to the questions are **yes** or **no**.

	Yes	No
1 Did the primary school children collect more rubbish than the teenagers?		
2 Does Ninetta want the government to change the law?		
3 Do Ninetta's friends think that what she is doing is dangerous?		
4 Were there any organisations interested in helping them on the beach?		
5 Was Ninetta annoyed about the broken glass?		

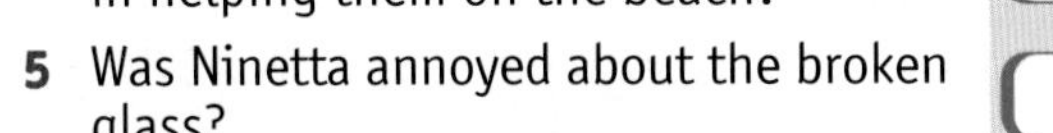

Speaking Link 

K Work with a partner. Discuss these questions.

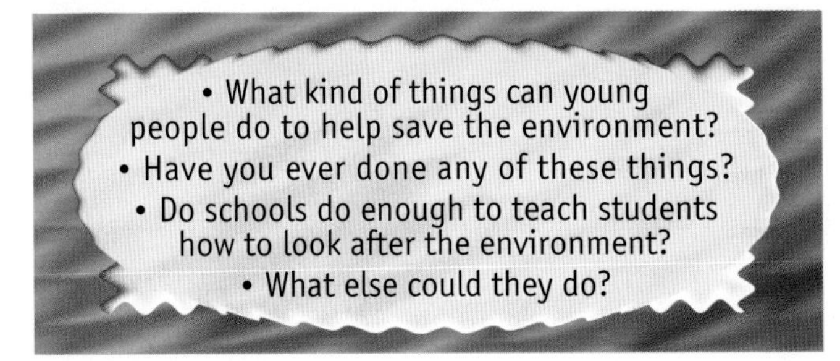

Now report back to the class.

Writing Link 

L *Imagine that you have spent a weekend doing one of the activities that you talked about in the Speaking Link. You want to write a letter to an English-speaking friend of yours who is studying in another town in your country. Tell him/her about what you have been doing recently, and describe your 'environment weekend'.*

Look at the outline below and then put the letter opposite in the correct order.

Letter Outline

Greeting	Dear (Mike)
Paragraph 1	Thank your friend for his/her letter and/or apologise for taking so long to write. (You could also comment on something he/she told you in his/ her last letter).
Paragraph 2	Tell your friend what you have been doing recently in general.
Paragraph 3	Describe the 'environment weekend'.
Closing paragraph	Ask your friend what he/she has being doing recently. Say that you are looking forward to hearing from him/her.
Signing off	Love/Best wishes (Tina)

A ☐

Last weekend I went to the beach with my school. When we got there, we started cleaning up the rubbish. On Sunday we had to actually go in the sea to get the rubbish out. At first nobody wanted to go in because it was freezing, but soon we were all splashing about! It was good fun, but hard work too!

B ☐

Love
Tina

C ☐

Dear Mike

D ☐

I finished my exams two weeks ago, and passed everything. Now that the exams are over, I have much more free time, so I've joined the local gym.

E ☐

Thanks for your letter. I was glad to hear that you did well in your exams. I'm sorry it's taken so long to write, but I've been really busy.

F ☐

What have you been up to? Write soon with all your news.

M Now write your letter, using the outline and the example to help you. Remember to use some of the expressions you learnt in Unit 1. (100-120 words)

HINTS

Don't forget that you are writing to a friend. He/She wants to know what you have been doing, so you must make it as interesting as possible. Use some of the adjectives you have learnt in this unit to describe your 'environment weekend'.

Review 2

Complete the following letter by putting **one** word in each space.

Dear Andrea

I know it ***(1)*** ....has........ *been a long time* ***(2)*** .... *I last wrote to you, but I* ***(3)*** .... *been busy recently. The work we have to do is* ***(4)*** .... *hard and I sometimes think that I am* ***(5)*** .... *stupid to be at university.*

Anyway, let me tell you what I have ***(6)*** .... *doing apart from work. I joined a couple of clubs last month. First I became a member of the Ecological Society, which is far more serious* ***(7)*** .... *I expected. The society* ***(8)*** .... *started by university students a few years ago and it has made quite a big difference to the local environment. The second club I joined was the football club. Don't laugh! I know you told me I wouldn't be good* ***(9)*** .... *to play here but I am just as good* ***(10)*** .... *anyone else in the club. I might even* ***(11)*** .... *chosen to play in the second team because several players* ***(12)*** .... *injured at the moment.*

That's all for now. Please write soon.

Best wishes
Pete

PS *Those old books I* ***(13)*** .... *been waiting for finally arrived last week. You can see them when I visit you in the holidays.*

Use the word in bold and other words to complete the second sentence, so that it has a similar meaning to the first one.

1 A weather satellite sends important information to meteorologists.
is
Important information ....is sent to........ ....meteorologists by.... a weather satellite.

2 This lake is too dirty to swim in.
enough
This lake .... to swim in.

3 The floods did a lot of damage.
was
A lot of damage .... the floods.

4 Some people say the island of Santorini isn't as popular as Mykonos.
more
Some people say the island of Mykonos .... Santorini.

5 The last time it snowed here was in 1985.
since
It .... 1985.

6 We didn't find the result very surprising.
by
We .... the result.

7 The first time we saw such a bad storm was in 1996.
never
We .... such a bad storm before 1996.

Match the words and phrases to make new expressions.

1	acid	f	a	beach	1	acid rain
2	ask		b	disaster	2	
3	crowded		c	surface	3	
4	natural		d	famous	4	
5	pass		e	questions	5	
6	predict		f	rain	6	
7	rubbish		g	scientist	7	
8	the earth's		h	dump	8	
9	weather		i	the time	9	
10	world		j	the weather	10	

Now complete the sentences below with the expressions from task C.

1 As well as being a ....world-famous.......... artist, he is also well known as a record-holder for the local cross country championships.

2 House developers wouldn't build near the .... because they believed no one would buy the houses.

3 You cannot .... just by listening to what old people tell you.

4 The heavy flooding in the UK is the biggest .... the country has seen since the beginning of the century.

5 The hotel we stayed at was near a .... so we went swimming in the pool.

6 My father works as a .... at the Meteorological Office.

7 I took plenty of magazines with me to .... on the flight to Australia.

8 .... is a serious environmental problem which damages plants and soil.

9 Some famous athletes don't like it when reporters .... them lots of ....

10 .... consists of about 70% water and 30% land.

A Are you a fitness fan or a couch potato? Do this questionnaire to find out! When you have finished, turn to page 119 for the results.

1 It's a school holiday. You
- **a** arrange a game of basketball or football with your friends.
- **b** play computer games all day.
- **c** go out for a coffee with your friends.

2 How often do you exercise? (Out of school hours!)
- **a** once a week
- **b** two or three times a week
- **c** rarely

Reading Link

B If your excuse for getting such a bad score in the questionnaire is that you don't have enough time or you are too tired, read on!

SCHOOL ADVISORY BOARD

Part One
What should you do when you feel exhausted?

Do you feel tired all the time? Well, you will be glad to hear that you're not alone. In a recent survey, students said that they were too tired. Don't worry though, help is at hand. Here are some facts about what can make you feel tired, and what you can do to avoid it.

1
You may think that lying in bed until 12 o'clock at the weekend is good for you, but you are wrong. Your biological clock tells you when you are tired. It also tells you when to wake up, and if you upset this by sleeping late at the weekend, it gets confused and you feel even more tired. A particular chemical is responsible for waking you up. It starts to work from 3 or 4 am until 11 am. If you sleep any later than this, you prevent the chemical from working, which in turn prevents you from feeling wide awake.

2
You may wonder what being thirsty has to do with being tired, but when you exercise or play a sport, it is very important that you drink enough. You feel thirsty because you have lost liquid from your body, and even with a loss of 3%, your physical ability is affected. You should drink at least 8 glasses of water a day.

3
Are you worried about your school marks? Well, don't be. That could be what is making you feel tired. When you are afraid, you tense your muscles, which causes extreme tiredness. Try to keep calm, and don't let things upset you. Close your eyes and take a deep breath. And remember, nothing is as bad as it seems!

4
The fact that you feel tired may be related to your diet. For example, eating ONLY carbohydrates makes you feel sleepy because the body produces a chemical which calms you down. Proteins, on the other hand, cause the body to produce another chemical, which wakes you up. Dieticians recommend we eat one portion of food which is high in protein at every meal.

5
Human beings are not like some animals. We are supposed to be awake during the day, and asleep at night. Most lights in our houses are brighter than they should be. Doctors say that the brain gets confused as it thinks you should be wide awake when you should really be fast asleep. Try to avoid very bright lights just before you go to bed. One simple solution is to install a special switch that enables you to choose exactly how bright you would like the light to be.

6
This is one you probably wish you could hear more often! When you study for a long time, your eyes can't see properly. As a result, you change positions and sit uncomfortably, which can make you feel tired. Make sure you take a short break from your work every hour, but remember to do something which does not strain your eyes. Make a (short!) phone call, or take the dog for a walk.

3 Your aunt gives you some money for your birthday. You
   a buy some new clothes for a party.
   b buy tickets for a football/basketball match.
   c buy a new tennis racket/basketball/snowboard.

4 How often do you eat fast food?
   a once a week
   b rarely
   c never

5 Which of the following do you like? (You may choose as many as you like.)
   a fruit
   b vegetables
   c freshly squeezed juice
   d milk

C Now match the headings with paragraphs 1-6 in the leaflet. There is one extra heading which will not be used.

A	Keep your cool	
B	Don't work too hard	
C	You are what you eat	
D	Find a balance	
E	Turn it down	
F	Don't try to catch up	
G	Drink up	

Vocabulary Link

D Find words or phrases in the leaflet which mean:

1 very tired (introduction)
....
2 change a situation, causing problems (para 1)
....
3 water or juice, for example; not solid (para 2)
....
4 make tight or stiff (para 3)
....
5 makes you quieter (para 4)
....
6 amount of food for one person (para 4)
....
7 cannot think clearly (para 5)
....
8 put in (para 5)
....
9 use too much; overuse (para 6)
....

E Complete the sentences with a form of the word in capitals. All the words are in the leaflet.

1 When you are healthy, your .... clock gives you the right signals at the right time. ***BIOLOGY***

2 A person who advises you about your food is called a .... ***DIET***

3 Choosing the right food to eat .... you to stay fit and healthy. ***ABLE***

4 She had sat .... on the old plastic chair for over three hours listening to the patients' complaints. ***COMFORTABLE***

5 It's difficult to feel wide .... when you have only had three hours' sleep. ***WAKE***

6 Do you know how many chemicals your body .... every day? ***PRODUCT***

7 Even old people have the .... to run long distances. ***ABLE***

8 The sun is .... than you think – don't forget to wear your sunglasses. ***BRIGHT***

F Match the problems with the possible causes.

Problems	Causes
1 fast pulse rate	*flu*
2 high temperature	*skin disease*
3 out of breath	*heart attack*
4 pain where my leg joins my foot	*a cold*
5 sore throat	*asthma*
6 spots	*sprained ankle*

Grammar Link

Reported Speech – Statements

Read this sentence taken from the leaflet.

In a recent survey, ***students said that they were too tired.***

Is this an example of direct speech or reported speech?

....

How do you know?

....

What tense is the reporting word **say** in?

....

What were the students' actual words?

....

Remember

To change from direct to reported speech you need to make changes to the form of the verb. Look at these and other changes in the Grammar Reference on pages 106 and 107 before you do the tasks.

G Read the dialogue and then change the sentences in bold into reported speech.

Helen	Let's go shopping. **My toes are almost sticking out of my trainers.**
Jane	Yes, my trainers are not in very good shape, either. **A new shop will be opening in the High Street on Saturday.** Shall we go then?
Helen	But it's only Monday, today. **My feet were hurting all day yesterday.**
Jane	Well, let's go to another shop, but **I must get back in time to go to the gym.**
Helen	**I know what I'm looking for**, so we won't be long.
Jane	OK, let's go.

1 Helen said ....
....

2 Jane said ....
....
....

3 Helen said ....
....
....

4 Jane said ....
....

5 Helen said ....
....

H Change the following statements into reported speech. Begin with the words given.

1 'I'll see you when I finish my workout,' said Bob.
Bob said ....
....

2 'Don't stop dieting until you have lost eight kilos,' said the dietician.
The dietician told me ....
....

3 'I must start eating healthier food,' said Tamsin.
Tamsin said ....
....

4 'I'm sorry that I spoke rudely to the doctor,' said Brenda.
Brenda apologised ....
....

5 'We can't explain what happened during training,' said the twins.
The twins told us ....
....

6 'Let's do some warm up exercises first,' said Eric.
Eric suggested ....
....

7 'I'm sure Sheila would have helped Jack if she had known about his weight problem,' said Nigel.
Nigel said ....
....
....

8 'You took all the vitamin pills, Stephanie,' said Olga.
Olga accused Stephanie ....
....

Speaking Link

I Work with a friend to ask and answer these questions.

- Are you fit?
- How often do you exercise?
- Are you a member of a gym, or do you go to a local sports centre?
- Do you believe that you lead a healthy lifestyle?
- Why is being fit and healthy important?
- What would you say to a friend who asked you what to do to get into shape?

Why don't you ...?
How about (trying) ...?
If I were you, I would (try) ... .
Have you thought about (eating) ...?
I think you should ... .

Listening Link 

J Listen to people talking in different situations and answer the questions below by choosing **a**, **b** or **c**.

> **HINTS**
>
> Before you listen, look at the questions to see what you should be listening for:
>
> - function – what something is used for, when it is used or why it is used;
> - location – where something is;
> - role – what someone does and
> - relationship – who someone is connected to.
>
> This will help you to choose the right information from the dialogues.

1. You hear this conversation on a bus. What does the man use his stick for?
   - **a** playing golf
   - **b** moving his shoes
   - **c** hitting his dog
2. Listen to this conversation between a woman and a doctor. Where are her son's spots?
   - **a** on his back
   - **b** at the top of his arm
   - **c** behind his ears
3. You hear a man speaking on the telephone. The person he is speaking to is his
   - **a** boss.
   - **b** son.
   - **c** doctor.
4. Listen to two friends talking. Why does one of them say, 'Don't worry, it's not serious.'
   - **a** She is trying to sympathise.
   - **b** She wants to help.
   - **c** She's being polite.
5. Listen to this man talking and decide who he is.
   - **a** a builder
   - **b** an engineer
   - **c** a dentist
6. Listen to a man giving a woman directions to the gymnasium. What is the quickest way to get there?
   - **a** on foot and by train
   - **b** by train
   - **c** by bus and train

Writing Link 

K *Imagine that you have received a letter from an English-speaking friend of yours. He/She has asked you for advice about getting into shape and eating healthy food. Write a letter to him/her, giving practical advice on fitness and healthy eating.*

Before you write your letter, complete the outline below.

Say that you are looking forward to his/her next letter, telling you all his/her news.

Thank your friend for his/her letter and say that you will try to help.

Love/Best wishes (Sam)

Dear (John)

Give your friend advice about eating healthy food.

Say that you hope you have been helpful and wish your friend good luck with his/her healthy lifestyle.

Letter Outline

Greeting	....
Paragraph 1	....
Paragraph 2	*Give your friend advice about getting into shape.*
Paragraph 3	....
Closing paragraph	....
Signing off	....

L Now write your letter, using some of the expressions from the Speaking Link, and the outline you completed in task K. (120 - 140 words)

Unit 10 Public Services

A Do you know how much extra people expect to be paid for giving good service? Choose the amount you think taxi drivers and waiters in these countries expect to get as a tip.

nothing
5-10%
11-15%
16-20%
more than 20%

Reading Link

B Read the information sheet below and say how many services are offered by the Discovery Centre.

Lesley Walker's Discovery Centre (LWDC)

Entertainment and Education Service for Young Children and Teenagers

Are you new in town? Or just bored? Then LWDC is the place for you. We specialise in services for young children and teenagers. Come and visit us in your free time and discover what is missing from your life.

R U Healthy?

Meet our fitness robot who will take your temperature, weigh you and measure your height. R U Healthy will also answer your questions about diet and personal relationships. The health centre is run by experienced staff who are used to working with young people.

Fame at Last!

Have your teachers ever asked if you wanted to get behind a microphone and give your opinion? Then now is your chance to learn some basic techniques about recording and news reporting. If you enjoy films, then come and learn how to make a video. All instructions are given by professional teachers who will also inform you about courses available at local schools and colleges.

Science and History Park

Learn about how people lived centuries ago and have fun experimenting with simple machines and microscopes in the science laboratory. Costumes are available for kids who want to experience a day in the life of King Arthur, for example. Science kits can be bought at competitive prices in the Centre's shop.

Design Studio

Test your creative abilities in our studio. Equipment and materials are available for the young artist, photographer or fashion designer. The latest computer technology helps you improve your work and techniques.

Children's Camp

Parents asked us where children could play in safety. We told them we have our own Pooh Bear Babysitting Service and a tree house village where kids can spend the day playing and using their imagination. A mini supermarket and mini restaurant have been specially built for our young customers.

Where to find us

Lesley Walker's Discovery Centre is in the heart of the historic gardens of Copham, close to suburban rail and bus connections. Free transport goes from the city centre to the gardens every 20 minutes. There are parking areas at the centre for bicycles, motorbikes and cars.

Hours

During the school term we are open on week days from 3 pm to 10 pm. During the holidays and weekends we open from 10 am to 10 pm.

Entrance

Children under 12 get in free of charge. 13 to 19-year-olds pay a fee of £20 for three months' worth of unlimited visits. Children under the age of 10 must bring an older brother or sister (or an adult) with them. Adults who come with their children enter free. Adults visiting on their own pay £5 for every visit. Everyone must apply for our special membership card.

Special Facilities

LWDC provides easy entrance everywhere for people in wheelchairs. All video presentations have text for people who are deaf or who have hearing difficulties. A sign language service is also available, but must be requested three days before you visit the centre.

Money for producing this information sheet has been given by Copham City Council and the Lesley Walker Children's Foundation.

Countries	Taxi Drivers	Waiters
1 Australia		
2 Belgium		
3 Canada		
4 Greece		
5 Italy		
6 Japan		
7 South Africa		
8 Switzerland		
9 The USA		

Were you right? Turn to page 119 for the right answers.

C Complete the sentences or answer the questions below by choosing from **a**, **b**, **c** or **d**.

1 Who takes care of the health service at the centre?

a R U Healthy
b adult staff
c the fitness robot
d young people

2 What does *experimenting with* mean in paragraph 3?

a using something to see how it works
b experiencing something to see how it feels
c having knowledge of something
d using something that scientists use

3 What does *where* refer to in line 7, paragraph 5?

a a tree house village
b Pooh Bear Babysitting Service
c spend the day playing
d using their imagination

4 In order to get to the Discovery Centre you have to

a take a 20-minute walk.
b go by bicycle, motorbike or car.
c walk through some gardens.
d take a bus from the city centre.

5 How much does it cost for a 10-year-old child to go to the centre with his parents?

a nothing
b £5
c £10
d £20

Vocabulary Link

D Circle the word that completes the sentences correctly.

1 In my **empty / free** time, I go to the library.
2 They are used to working **with / together** young children.
3 The new postage stamps will only be available **with / for** collectors.
4 The post office is a **10-minute / 10 minutes** walk from the bus stop.
5 The policeman is paid quite a low **fee / salary** for such a dangerous job.
6 The bank has given me £30 **value / worth** of cheques.
7 You can get into the cinema **free of charge / free entrance** on Wednesday evening.
8 The Town Hall provides wooden benches **for / to** its senior citizens.

E Match the words to make complete phrases. There may be more than one possible answer.

1 save	a a bank account
2 post	b money
3 make	c a cheque
4 write	d a waiter
5 open	e a phone call
6 toss	f a coin
7 tip	g a letter

F Complete the sentences below with the complete phrases from task E. In some cases you will have to change the form.

1 Jennifer is trying to .... for her holiday.
2 The doctor .... and the ambulance arrived very quickly.
3 The manager said I couldn't .... until I was 18.
4 She .... because he had served her with a smile.
5 If you .... to Mary today, it will reach her on Monday.
6 The man from the insurance company refused to .... to pay for the damage to my car.
7 If you don't know who should start first, let's .... to decide.

Grammar Link

Reported Speech – Questions

Read the following sentence from the text.

*Parents **asked us where children could play** in safety.*

Which reporting verb is used here? ....
What kind of word comes after the question word (*who, what, when* etc.)? ....

Now read this sentence from the text.

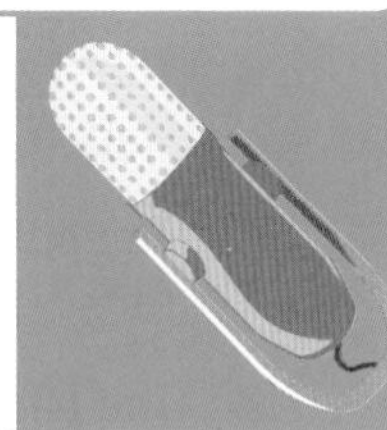

*Have your teachers ever **asked if you wanted** to get behind a microphone and give your opinion?*

What word is used when there is no question word?
....

Study the Grammar Reference on page 108 before you do the task.

G Change the following spoken questions into reported speech.

1 'Did you take the books back to the library, Mel?' asked Angus.
Angus asked Mel ....
....

2 'Where have you put the stamps, Malcolm?' asked Jackie.
Jackie asked Malcolm ....
....

3 'When are you going to post the cards, Mark?' asked Yvonne.
Yvonne asked Mark ....
....

4 'How long will it take for the parcel to reach Sydney?' asked John.
John wanted to know....................................
....

5 'Does it cost a lot to send a postcard to Canada?' asked Carol.
Carol wanted to know ....
....

6 'Where is the nearest post office?' asked the boy.
The boy asked me ....
....

7 'How much can we put in our account every month, Cathy?' asked Oliver.
Oliver asked Cathy ....
....

Listening Link

H Listen to the telephone conversation between a teenager and the secretary of the Discovery Centre. Fill in the missing information on the form in the spaces provided.

LESLEY WALKER'S DISCOVERY CENTRE (LWDC)
Entertainment and Education Service for Young Children and Teenagers

Application for Membership

Name: (1) ....*Barnes*.

(2) Adult ☐ Teenager ☐ Child ☐

Address: (3) ..*6*.............................*Close*....
Newtown..

Telephone: (4) ....

Date of Birth (for children and teenagers):
(5) ....

(6) New Member ☐ Renew Membership ☐

Membership Number: (7) | J | B | M | | | | | P | Q |

(8) Services required:
Health Check ☐
Pooh Bear Babysitting Service ☐
Special Needs: wheelchair ☐
video text ☐
sign language ☐

Fee:
(9) full rate ☐ reduced rate ☐ free entrance ☐

Date: (10) ....*2000*..........

Speaking Link

I Look at the photographs and talk about their similarities and differences.

A

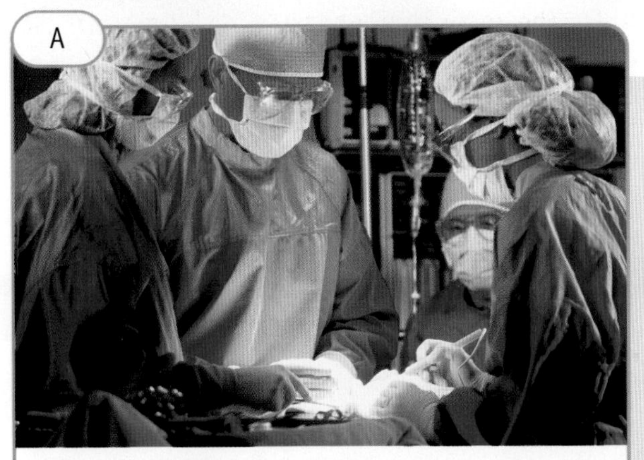

operating theatre, surgeons, gowns, masks, drip

B

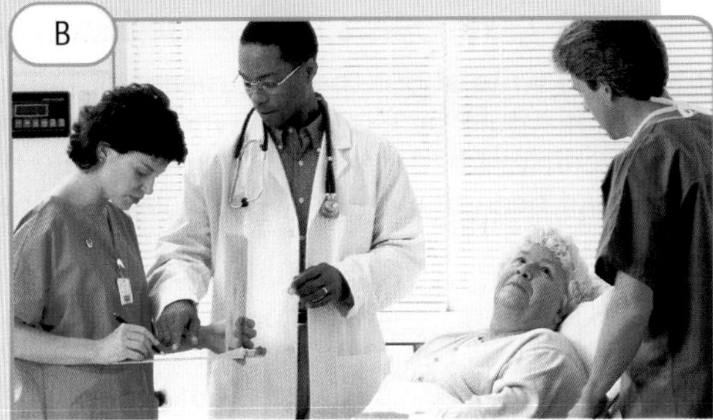

hospital ward, doctor, surgeon, nurse, patient's chart, stethoscope

- Would you expect to see the same situations in a hospital in your country?

Writing Link

In this unit you are going to learn how to write a composition which gives suggestions or solutions to a problem.

J Look at the question below and the outline opposite and separate the model composition into four paragraphs.

Imagine that you read this notice on a hospital noticeboard when you went there to visit a friend, and you have decided to enter the competition. Read the notice carefully and write your composition.

St David's Hospital
COMPETITION

DO YOU WANT TO WIN
A BRAND NEW COMPUTER?

All you have to do is write a composition in approximately 120 words, saying what you think can be done to improve the Health Service in your country.

One of the biggest problems in our country is the Health Service. It is very difficult to improve, but there are some things that the government can do. First of all, there aren't enough doctors and nurses in the hospitals in my country. However, there are lots of unemployed doctors and nurses, so the government could easily employ more hospital staff. Another point is that there aren't enough local health centres. It is very difficult for some people, such as the elderly, to go a long way to visit the doctor. This problem could be solved if there were local health centres in all areas. To sum up, the Health Service is far from perfect and could be improved greatly if the government took some measures.

Composition Outline

Paragraph 1	Introduce the problem and say that it can be solved.
Paragraphs 2 and 3	For each main paragraph write a topic sentence to introduce one particular part of the problem, and suggest a solution. Give examples to support your ideas.
Paragraph 4	Summarise your main points and give a thought for the future. Try to be optimistic.

K Underline the words or phrases which helped you to separate the composition into paragraphs.

L Now write your own composition, using your own ideas, the outline and some of the expressions here. (120-140 words)

Helpful Expressions

First of all, ...
One of the biggest problems is ...
Another point is ...
What is more, ...
To sum up, ...

A Match the ways of travelling with the means of transport.

1 by air
2 by rail
3 by sea
4 by road

Reading Link

B Read through the article and say how many means of transport the writer talks about. Check your list with a friend.

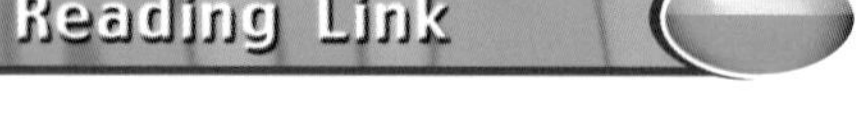

Ordinary Traveller

Special report by Simon Jackson

When I was first asked to write about the best means of transport in the world, I thought it would be easy. But when I was told that I could only choose vehicles I had personally travelled by, I had to think carefully about what I had been doing from when I was a teenager to the present time. **1**

My favourite train, for example, is thought to be the best in the world, so I had little difficulty in choosing it. As well as being my favourite, *The Blue Train* is also the pride of South Africa's railways. **2** One travels between Pretoria and Cape Town while the other travels between Pretoria and Victoria Falls. A few years ago, my wife and I spent two nights on board the Victoria Falls train, paying a fare of just over £1000 each. The 380-metre-long train has 18 carriages, where 84 passengers and 27 staff can stay comfortably. It was a unique experience and one I could happily repeat.

A more difficult choice was that of my favourite motorbike. **3** However, that changed last week when a friend bought a new Yamaha YZF-R1. It was, as I found out, extremely fast. My friend let me test the bike, even though I wasn't used to riding such a fast bike, and I was amazed to discover how well it performed.

Perhaps the hardest choice to make was that of my favourite car. Aston Martins, Ferraris and Porsches didn't count because I have never driven any of them. Instead, I chose a 1962 Rover 75 which my father used to drive. **4** It was neither fast nor easy to handle. But I liked its leather seats and its 'character' – something which seems to be missing in modern vehicles.

I have only ever been on one cruise so my choice of ship was easy. When I graduated from university, the *Azur* was my home for five days when I went on a cruise round the Mediterranean. I had a cabin on one of the upper decks, which was very comfortable. Unfortunately, five days was not enough time for me to get used to this luxury. **5** There were also organised tours at each port.

Finally, air travel for me is almost always the same. **6** It is for this reason that I chose a Cessna which was owned by a pilot I used to know. Because it was so small, it really gave me a sense of freedom and an idea of how it must have felt in the early days of flying.

C The following sentences have been removed from the article.
Read through the article and put each sentence in the correct place.

A Until recently I would have chosen the old Triumph Bonneville that has stood in my garage for almost 30 years.

B He would polish it regularly and would even make sure that it was dry before leaving it in the garage after a journey in the rain.

C You sit in a departure lounge, get on board, wait for the plane to take off, have a meal and fall asleep in your aisle or window seat.

D There are, in fact, two of them and not one as the name might suggest.

E As well as the comfort, there were plenty of activities available during the day followed by a programme of entertainment at night.

F Fortunately, some decisions were easy to make because my opinion is also shared by others.

Vocabulary Link

D The words and phrases below have been taken from the article. Choose the word or phrase closest in meaning to each one.

1 vehicles (para 1)	a means of transport b ways of driving
2 pride (para 2)	a satisfaction b the most valuable thing
3 fare (para 2)	a a train ticket b the price charged to travel
4 carriage (para 2)	a a machine b part of a train
5 performed (para 3)	a played b worked
6 handle (para 4)	a touch b control
7 graduated (para 5)	a left university with a degree b completed my education
8 upper decks (para 5)	a more expensive parts b higher floors on a ship
9 was owned by (para 6)	a was kept by b belonged to
10 sense (para 6)	a feeling b ability

E Match the phrasal verbs in the sentences with the explanations.

1 The airline asked us to **check in** two hours before departure. ☐	a climb or step onto
2 The bus drivers were on strike, so we **set off** for school on foot. ☐	b started on a journey
3 The car **ran out of** petrol in the middle of nowhere. ☐	c left the ground
4 The inspector made the old lady **get off** the train because she didn't have a ticket. ☐	d report your arrival and leave your luggage
5 People were trying to **get on** the bus even though the driver had closed the doors. ☐	e leave the vehicle
6 The plane **took off** nearly one hour late. ☐	f had none left

F Complete the sentences with the phrasal verbs from task E. Make sure you use the correct form of the verb.

1. The plane .... in the middle of a huge thunderstorm.
2. When the man tried to .... at the hotel, he was told that there were no empty rooms.
3. The two teenagers .... on the journey of a lifetime.
4. You should carry a plastic container in your car in case you .... petrol.
5. The man .... the train and slipped on a banana skin on the platform.
6. I couldn't .... the plane, because I had lost my boarding card.

used to, would

Read these two sentences taken from the article.

*Instead, I chose a 1962 Rover 75 which my father **used to** drive.*

*He **would** polish it regularly and **would** even make sure that it was dry ...*

Do **used to** and **would** talk about the present or past?

....

Remember

Used to and **would** are followed by verbs without **to**. The negative form of **used to** is **didn't use to**.

be used to / get used to

Read this sentence from the article.

*My friend let me test the bike even though I **wasn't used to** riding such a fast bike ...*

*Unfortunately, five days was not enough time for me **to get used to** this luxury.*

What form of the verb follows **be / get used to**?

....

Do **be / get used to** have to be followed by a verb?

....

Now complete the following rule.

Be / get used to can be followed by either a verb in the .... form, or a ....

Study the Grammar Reference on page 108 before you do the task.

G Complete the following sentences by putting the verbs in brackets in the correct form.

1. It was difficult at first but I soon got used to .... (work) for the bus company.
2. She used to .... (travel) all over the country.
3. My mother would .... (take) me for a train ride on my birthday when I was young.
4. Sam isn't used to .... (drive) around a small village.
5. Don't worry! You'll soon get used to .... (go) long distances by car.
6. We get used to .... (walk) when the bus drivers go on strike.
7. I didn't use to .... (like) flying when I was younger.
8. He was used to .... (run) the transport museum so he knew how to manage staff.

Listening Link

H You will hear four different people talking about driving cars. Choose from the list (**a-e**) to show which opinion each speaker has. There is one extra letter which you won't need to use.

- **a** Motorists are irresponsible, careless and impatient.
- **b** Cars cause pollution and damage our historic buildings.
- **c** It's the cheapest, fastest way to get around.
- **d** Driving at speed is fun – in the right place, of course.
- **e** There are not enough parking spaces in town.

Speaker 1	☐	Speaker 3	☐
Speaker 2	☐	Speaker 4	☐

Speaking Link 

I Work with a partner. Look at the plan of a town. There are three areas marked **A**, **B** and **C** which are possible sites for an airport. Imagine that you work for the town council, and you must decide which area is the best site for the airport. Remember, you must give reasons for your answers.

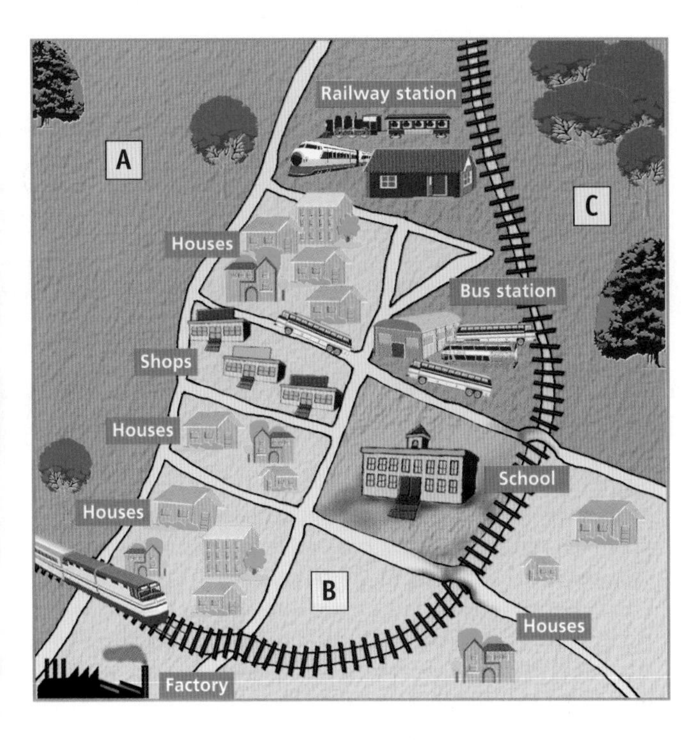

You can use the expressions you learnt in Units 3 and 7 to help you.

Now report back to the class. Which was the most popular site for the airport?

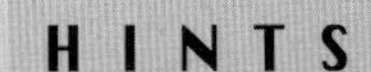

HINTS

It is a good idea to give reasons why the other options are not suitable before you talk about what you think is the best option.

Writing Link 

In Unit 2, you learnt how to write a description of a person. In this unit, you are going to learn how to write a description of a place.

J Read the question below and the model opposite, then add any punctuation or capital letters necessary. The outline will help you to separate the description into paragraphs.

Imagine that as part of a school project on transport, your teacher has asked your class to write compositions on the following subject: Describe a memorable visit to an airport.

i shall never forget the time i spent ten hours at londons heathrow airport when my flight was delayed due to bad weather conditions having checked in my first stop was the departure lounge most people looked nervous as if this flight would be their last there were also some noisy teenagers and tired mothers screaming at their children it was far too noisy there so i let the smell of fresh coffee guide me to a cafe near the duty-free shop i watched people pushing trolleys piled high with suitcases holding plastic bags with their duty-free purchases i soon got bored so i went upstairs to the flight gallery the planes looked like giant birds taking off and coming in to land i decided that this was the most peaceful spot in the airport and i waited patiently for my flight to be announced

Description Outline

Paragraph 1	Let the reader know why you have chosen your topic.
Paragraphs 2 and 3	Describe the airport, choosing a few interesting details.
Paragraph 4	Finish off your composition in a natural way.

HINTS

- When you are describing something, no matter what it is, you should remember to use all your senses, not just your sense of sight. For example, when you are describing a place, you can describe what you smell and hear as well as what you see.
- You should try to use vocabulary related to the place you are describing.
- Use colourful, imaginative language when you are describing something. The use of adjectives can make a description more interesting.

K Now write your own description, using your own ideas. (120-140 words)

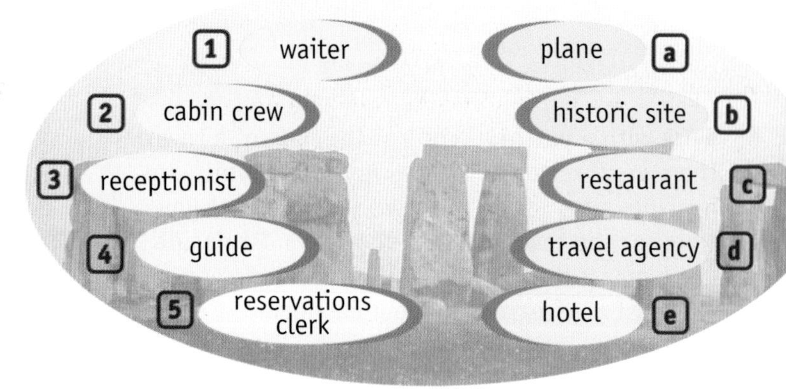

A Match the people with the place you would be most likely to find them in.

Reading Link

B Read through the traveller's diary and work with a friend to make a list of the things she saw on the journey.

Coast to Coast

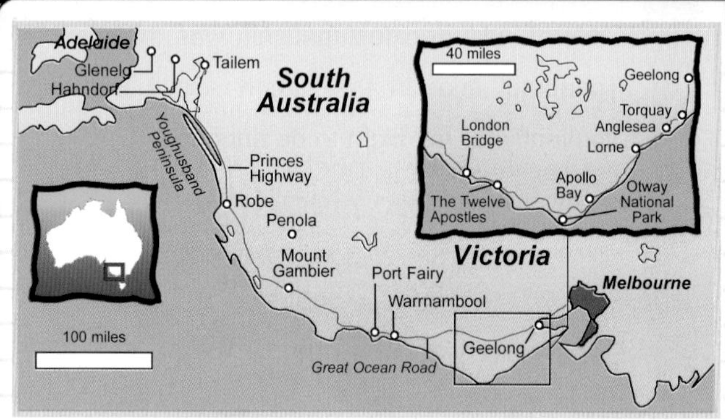

A Day One: Thursday 9th, Adelaide

I got to Adelaide on a direct flight from Heathrow with Qantas, the Australian airline. On arrival in Adelaide, I hired a mini-camper van for $120 a day. The price included insurance, cooking facilities and bed linen. I also decided to buy a snake-bite kit in case I got bitten by one of Australia's many poisonous snakes.

B Day Two: Friday 10th, Adelaide to Coorong

Leaving Adelaide, I headed inland towards Glenelg, an Australian holiday resort. Then I moved on to Hahndorf, a town where there is a strong German influence. From there, I crossed the Murray River and reached Tailem, where the road to Melbourne splits. You can take the slow road if you have time on your hands, but I made for Coorong National Park, which is a paradise for millions of birds, on the fast road.

C Day Three: Saturday 11th, Robe to Penola

The next place I visited was Robe, a peaceful fishing village which is slowly being filled with holiday homes. At Robe I left the sea for Penola. My bed for the night was in a cottage. I would probably have slept in the van if I had hired one with a toilet and shower facilities, but I was glad of the company, especially with deadly snakes around. I was so tired that I slept like a log.

D Day Four: Sunday 12th, South to Port Fairy

My next stop was at the town of Mount Gambier, which sits on the side of a volcano. Inside the crater is the Blue Lake where, for reasons scientists are unable to explain, the water changes colour according to the season. After a short visit, I continued down towards the coast. At Port Fairy, I met my guide, Noel, in the Tower Hill nature reserve. 'You'll see every kind of animal we have if you're quiet,' he said. He was right. I saw koalas, emus and kangaroos.

E Day Five: Monday 13th, The Shipwreck Coast

The name of this part of the coast comes from the large number of ships that ended their voyages on the rocky coastline. The howling winds and crashing waves smash into the rocks in winter, creating hundreds of caves and causing the coast to retreat.

F Day Six: Tuesday 14th, The Twelve Apostles

The Twelve Apostles is a group of tall, thin rocks sticking out of the sea. Once there were 13 of them, now there are ten. I could only see eight from the coast but I was told you could count all ten from the air. After gazing at this wonderful view, I headed for Melbourne and the end of the road.

G Day Seven: Wednesday 15th, On to Melbourne

After nearly a week on the road, we passed through the national park and meadows where we saw sheep and cows. The end of Geelong marks the end of the Great Ocean Road and the beginning of Melbourne. As I approached my destination, I saw a sign which read Shipwreck Coast. I thought to myself: 'I would drive back to Adelaide if I had the time, but along the slow road and not the way I came.'

C Answer the questions below by finding which part or parts (A-G) they refer to.

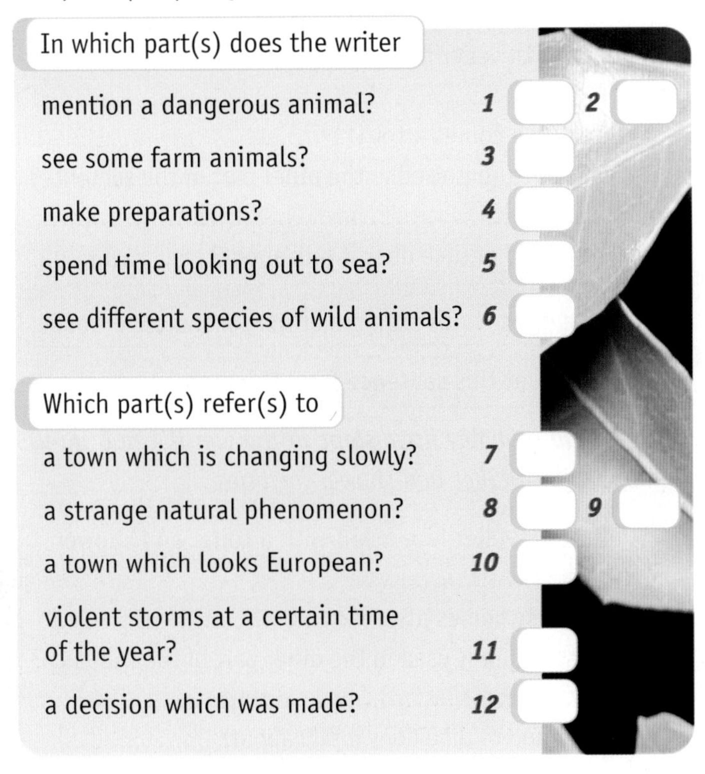

In which part(s) does the writer

mention a dangerous animal? **1** ___ **2** ___

see some farm animals? **3** ___

make preparations? **4** ___

spend time looking out to sea? **5** ___

see different species of wild animals? **6** ___

Which part(s) refer(s) to

a town which is changing slowly? **7** ___

a strange natural phenomenon? **8** ___ **9** ___

a town which looks European? **10** ___

violent storms at a certain time of the year? **11** ___

a decision which was made? **12** ___

Vocabulary Link

D The words and phrases below have been taken from the diary. Choose the word or phrase closest in meaning to each one.

1 direct flight (part A)	**a** without stopping **b** one-way
2 hired (part A)	**a** lifted up **b** rented
3 facilities (part A)	**a** equipment **b** abilities
4 splits (part B)	**a** separates **b** breaks
5 made for (part B)	**a** travelled round **b** went towards
6 deadly (part C)	**a** very serious **b** able to kill
7 guide (part D)	**a** book giving information **b** somebody who shows the way
8 retreat (part E)	**a** return **b** move back
9 gazing (part F)	**a** looking at **b** thinking about
10 destination (part G)	**a** journey's end **b** place to rest

E Can you place these idioms in the correct places in the sentences below?

dead tired · in single file · slept like a log · travel light · in high spirits · had butterflies in my stomach

1 I always .... because I don't like carrying heavy luggage.

2 Peter was .... after climbing for over eight hours.

3 I .... when I saw the snake heading in my direction.

4 The cottage was so peaceful that I ....

5 We started the journey ...., but after a 6-hour wait in the airport, we began to feel depressed.

6 We had to walk along the mountain path .... because it was so narrow.

Listening Link

F Listen to this news report about a hotel fire. For questions 1-5, decide which of the choices **a**, **b** or **c** is the correct answer.

1 Where was Tina Litherland when the fire started?
- **a** on the fourth floor
- **b** in her room
- **c** in the lift

2 What did the hotel guests do when the alarm went off?
- **a** They panicked and ran into the lifts.
- **b** They tried to run down the stairs.
- **c** They climbed out of the windows.

3 When was the hotel built?
- **a** in the last 10 years
- **b** over 20 years ago
- **c** nearly 50 years ago

4 How did the fire start?
- **a** There was an electrical problem.
- **b** Something caught fire in the kitchen.
- **c** A guest's cigarette burnt the carpet.

5 How many people were injured?
- **a** none
- **b** a few
- **c** one or two

Grammar Link

Conditionals

Read this sentence from the diary.

'*You'**ll see** every kind of animal we have **if** you'**re** quiet,' he said.*

What tense comes after **if**? ....
What tense is used at the beginning of the sentence?
....

This is another way to say the same sentence.

'***Unless** you **are** quiet, you **won't see** every kind of animal we have.*'

What period of time do they talk about? ....

These sentences are examples of the first conditional.

Now, read this sentence from the diary.

*I **would drive** back to Adelaide **if** I **had** the time ...*

Does the traveller have time to drive back to Adelaide?
....
What tense comes after **if**? ....
What structure is used in the other part of the sentence?
....
What period of time does it talk about? ....

This sentence is an example of the second conditional.

Now look at this sentence from the diary.

*I **would** probably **have slept** in the van **if I had hired** one with a toilet and shower facilities ...*

Did the traveller hire a van with a toilet and shower facilities? ....
What tense comes after **if**? ....
What structure is used in the other part of the sentence?
....
What period of time does it talk about? ....

This is an example of the third conditional.

Study the Grammar Reference on page 108 and 109 before you do to the tasks.

G Match the parts of the sentences.

1 I wouldn't travel alone
2 Mary will visit the old ship
3 If you take the old road,
4 If I were you,
5 He wouldn't drive there
6 If the snake wasn't poisonous,

a I would become a guide.
b if it doesn't rain.
c if he didn't have the time.
d unless I was in a really safe place.
e it would make a good pet.
f you will have a breathtaking view.

H Complete the following sentences by putting the verbs in brackets into the correct form.

1 I'll close the hotel if the tour operator ....(not pay) me what it owes me.
2 I .... (lend) you the car if you drive carefully.
3 If I'd had the chance to emigrate to New Zealand, I .... (not think) about it twice.
4 If I went on holiday to the Caribbean, some of my neighbours .... (be) jealous.
5 She wouldn't have flown there if it .... (not be) so urgent.
6 I would never hurt an animal unless it .... (attack) me first.
7 I .... (go) on a skiing holiday if I didn't have all these household expenses.

Speaking Link

I Work with a partner. Discuss these questions.

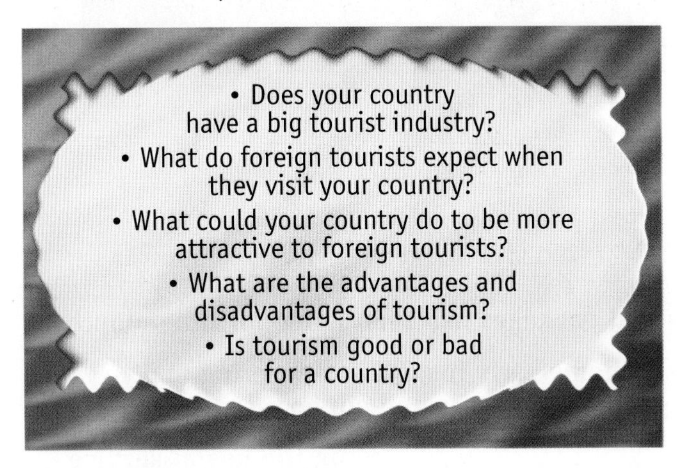

- Does your country have a big tourist industry?
- What do foreign tourists expect when they visit your country?
- What could your country do to be more attractive to foreign tourists?
- What are the advantages and disadvantages of tourism?
- Is tourism good or bad for a country?

Now report back to the class.

Writing Link

In Unit 3, you wrote a letter giving information and, in Unit 6, you wrote a letter asking for information. In this unit, you are going to learn how to write a letter asking for and giving information.

J Read the question, the advertisement and the letter and fill the gaps with the most suitable phrase from the box below the letter.

Imagine that you want to go on holiday to England this summer. You have seen an advertisement for a hotel in London, and you are interested in staying there. Before you make your final decision, you would like some more information. Look at the advertisement below, and write your letter to the hotel manager.

Dear Sir/Madam

I saw an advertisement for the Green Park Hotel in my local newspaper recently, and I am interested in staying there. (1) .... further information about your hotel.

My family and I will be in London from 20th July for fourteen nights. We would like one double room, and a single room for our son. We would like half board accommodation, and (2) .... the city tours mentioned in your advertisement.

(3) .... you could give me some further information. Firstly, (4) .... how much it will cost us? (5) .... if your hotel has a swimming pool or a gym.

I would like to thank you in advance for your assistance. (6) .... hearing from you.

Yours faithfully

Maria Pepe

Helpful Expressions

- a ... could you let me know ...
- b I would be grateful if ...
- c I look forward to ...
- d I am writing to ask for ...
- e I would also like to know ...
- f ... we are very interested in ...

K Now write your own letter, using your own ideas, and looking at the outline below. (120-140 words)

Letter Outline

Greeting	Dear Sir/Madam
Paragraph 1	Say where and when you saw the advertisement. Say why you are writing.
Paragraph 2	Give relevant information.
Paragraph 3	Ask for necessary information.
Closing paragraph	Give your thanks. Say that you are looking forward to their reply.
Signing off	Yours faithfully (your name)

Review 3

Complete the following article by putting **one** word in each space.

Lazy Postman Kept 15,000 Letters!

A lazy postman who failed to deliver 15,000 letters and packages has been jailed for nine months.

Richard Dunn, who (1) ....used.............. to go home early instead of delivering mail, (2) .... hide the letters in his garage, home, car and cupboard at work.

Judge Francis Allen, who blamed Dunn (3) .... giving the postal service a bad name, (4) .... the former postman that he (5) .... been extremely lazy and there was no alternative but a prison sentence.

Martin Jenkins, defending, said: 'Mr Dunn (6) .... used to going home early without being caught. Perhaps (7) .... an inspector had checked on him earlier, he (8) .... not have got away with it for so long.'

The judge (9) .... Dunn why he had started hiding mail, but the ex-postman, who now works as a tree surgeon, said that he (10) .... not know.

While summing up, Judge Allen said: 'The public are entitled to expect that their mail will be delivered and it WILL be if people like Dunn (11) .... not responsible for delivering it.'

Choose the correct alternative in each of the following sentences.

1. I am not used to **go / going** to work by bus.
2. I'll see a specialist if you **would come / come** with me.
3. They **told / said** me that the bank was closed.
4. Nathan used to **drive / driving** a lorry.
5. If I **didn't take / hadn't taken** a taxi, I would have been late.
6. The doctor asked me how long **had I been / I had been** having treatment for arthritis.
7. She would never **to complain / complain** even when she was in pain.
8. What kind of car would you buy if you **had / had had** a lot of money?
9. The travel agent suggested **me to go / I should go** by plane.
10. 'You'll soon get used to **eating / eat** healthy food,'said the doctor.

Use the words given in capitals at the end of each sentence to form a word that fits in the space.

1	The airline said they were not ......responsible...... for the delays at the airport.	RESPONSIBILITY
2	A travel agent needs the .... to match a customer's request with an appropriate holiday.	ABLE
3	The travel agency was offering .... prices for trips to Australia.	COMPETE
4	The marathon runner had breathing .... after the eleventh mile.	DIFFICULT
5	We were lucky to find a .... priced holiday at the last minute.	REASONABLE
6	................................, I don't think doctors are paid enough money.	PERSON
7	Be careful! The snakes and spiders in this area are	POISON
8	The .... park contains the most beautiful display of orchids in the world.	NATION
9	Your guide will be there to meet you when you reach your	DESTINED
10	My .... stamp is a Hungarian one with beautiful butterflies on it.	FAVOUR

In each line of the paragraph below, there is an extra word. Circle the word.

A Broken Bone

1 Last week I fell down the stairs and hurt myself so I (had) had to go to hospital. I had
2 broken a bone in my foot! My mother said me that if I had been more careful it wouldn't
3 have happened. In fact, it was nothing to do with being careful – the heel of my boot has had
4 broken. So, I have had to be get used to walking with the help of crutches. It's quite easy to get
5 around and if you don't have to climb stairs. I carry a plastic bag to school with me so
6 that if it rains, I can have cover the plaster on my foot. My brother told me it was a good
7 excuse to get others to help me. However, I know that unless I not get better soon, I won't be
8 able to play in the school basketball team. My teacher told to me to be patient!

Complete the sentences with a verb in the correct form.

1 If the plane doesn't ....take........... off soon, I'm going to complain.
2 Penny .... in two suitcases at the airport and only found one of them at her destination.
3 After the earthquake, the hospital .... out of bandages.
4 Don't .... off the bus until you reach the stop after the hospital.
5 Unless you .... off early in the morning, you won't see the wild geese.
6 I laughed when I saw a man trying to .... on the bus with a very tall plant.

Unit 13 Shopping

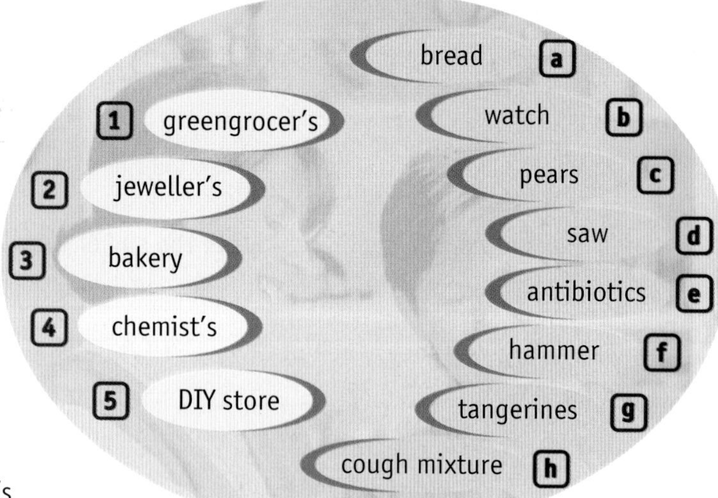

A Match the types of shop with the products that can be bought in them.

Reading Link

B Read this report and find three ways in which people's shopping habits have changed.

To: *Ms L Brown*
From: *R Webb*
Subject: *Shopping Habits*
Date: *23.5.2002*

1

Here is the report which shows how shopping habits are changing. Due to the long hours people work, it is no longer normal for a working day to be limited to eight hours in an office. Therefore, people are beginning to use 24-hour services. As a result, supermarket staff and other shop workers who used to work during traditional opening hours are now needed at any time of the day or night.

2

There are supermarkets whose doors are open around the clock. *Tesco*, which is one of the largest supermarket chains in Britain, never closes a quarter of its stores. It says that it is surprised at the number of grandmothers and mothers with small children who shop in the early hours of the morning. At the moment, the supermarkets that stay open are near motorways, but this will soon change. There are already some towns where even the smaller chains stay open for longer hours.

3

According to a survey carried out for *Abbey National*, three in four families buy ready-cooked meals regularly, typically costing £20 each week, because they cannot find the time to cook. The same survey found that three in five people buy food at expensive local shops because there is often no time to get to the supermarket.

4

Because of the changes in modern lifestyles, people need to be able to shop at all hours of the day. In future, many other shops and stores as well as supermarkets will be open all day and night. In short, we will become a 24-hour society.

C Now read this report and find out what shoppers suggest you do before you visit a supermarket.

Class Five Finds Out About Local Supermarket Shopping

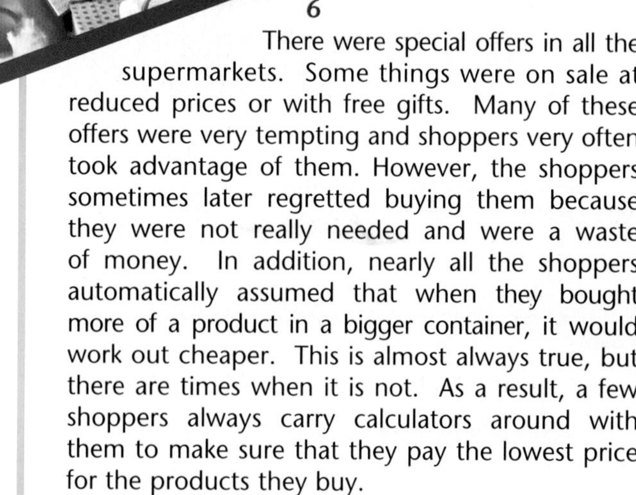

5

This report is based on interviews with 116 shoppers at four different, well-known, local supermarkets. The interviews took place in March, when people's shopping habits are not affected by the holiday seasons or the sales. The shoppers who were interviewed were aged between 19 and 75.

6

There were special offers in all the supermarkets. Some things were on sale at reduced prices or with free gifts. Many of these offers were very tempting and shoppers very often took advantage of them. However, the shoppers sometimes later regretted buying them because they were not really needed and were a waste of money. In addition, nearly all the shoppers automatically assumed that when they bought more of a product in a bigger container, it would work out cheaper. This is almost always true, but there are times when it is not. As a result, a few shoppers always carry calculators around with them to make sure that they pay the lowest price for the products they buy.

7

The majority of shoppers agreed that it is best to write down the things you need from the supermarket before you go shopping. They said you should not be tempted by bargains, free gifts or large containers unless you are absolutely sure that you need them.

D Read the reports again and match these headings with each part of the reports.

A	A changing society	
B	A wide variety of shoppers	
C	Shop around the clock	
D	Stick to a list	
E	No time to cook	
F	False economy	
G	Unexpected customers	

Vocabulary Link

E The words and phrases below have been taken from the reports. Circle the word or phrase closest in meaning to each one.

1	due to (part 1)	**a** except **b** because of
2	chains (part 2)	**a** staff **b** number of stores
3	survey (part 3)	**a** investigation **b** search
4	carried out (part 3)	**a** taken **b** done
5	reduced (part 6)	**a** lower **b** almost free
6	tempting (part 6)	**a** excellent **b** attractive
7	took advantage of (part 6)	**a** made the most of **b** made a profit
8	regretted (part 6)	**a** hated **b** were sorry about
9	assumed (part 6)	**a** supposed **b** decided

F Circle the word that completes the sentences correctly.

1. The assistant helped me find the right **pear / pair** of shoes.
2. The new shop **hours / ours** will start on Monday.
3. There are **eight / ate** legs on the old wooden table.
4. I feel **week / weak** after carrying all that shopping.
5. The cashier gave them **there / their** change.
6. Jenny didn't know what to **buy / by** for her aunt's birthday.
7. Who **would / wood** like to go to the supermarket with me?
8. How much is the **fare / fair** from here to the DIY store?

Listening Link

G Listen to people talking in different situations and answer the questions by choosing **a**, **b** or **c**.

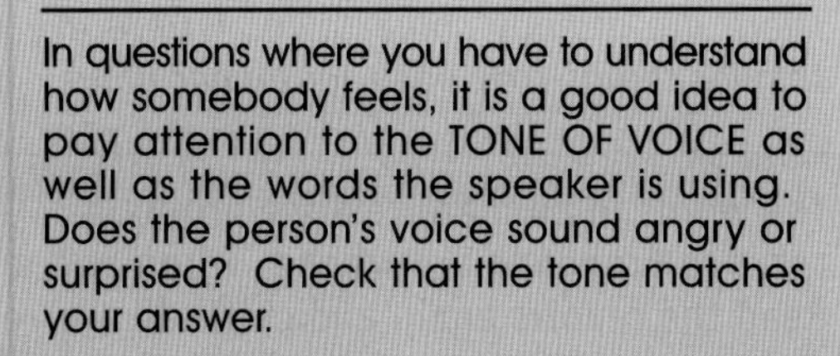

HINTS

In questions where you have to understand how somebody feels, it is a good idea to pay attention to the TONE OF VOICE as well as the words the speaker is using. Does the person's voice sound angry or surprised? Check that the tone matches your answer.

1. Listen to a man talking about his local supermarket. What is his attitude towards the cashiers?
   a positive
   b negative
   c neutral
2. You hear this woman talking to her new computer. How does she feel?
   a angry
   b stupid
   c helpless
3. You hear a couple having a discussion about their neighbours' new car. They believe their neighbours
   a should park it in their garage.
   b have stolen it from the garage.
   c can't afford to buy petrol for it.
4. You hear two men talking in the street. How does one of them feel about returning a new washing machine?
   a He's annoyed with his wife.
   b He believes the shop is wrong.
   c He wants to surprise his wife.
5. Two women are shouting in a shop. They are
   a angry.
   b surprised.
   c delighted.
6. A man is walking around the supermarket talking to himself. Why?
   a He can't find something on his shopping list.
   b He is unhappy because everything has been moved.
   c He is complaining because his wife sent him shopping.
7. You hear a man talking on a television programme about door-to-door sales people. What is his attitude towards them?
   a He thinks they are friendly.
   b He doesn't trust them at all.
   c He thinks they waste his time.

Grammar Link

Relative Clauses

Look at these examples from the reports.

The shoppers ***who*** *were interviewed were aged between 19 and 75.*

There are already some towns ***where*** *even the smaller chains stay open for longer hours.*

The words in bold are relative pronouns. Other relative pronouns are **whose**, **when** and **which**. Read the reports again and circle all the relative pronouns you find. Now complete the table below.

relative pronoun	talks about ...
who	
	things
	places
	possessives
when	

A relative pronoun comes at the beginning of a relative clause. A relative clause gives more information about the subject or object of a sentence. In some relative clauses the information is necessary and in others it is extra. Look at the Grammar Reference on page 109 for more information before you do the tasks.

H Complete the following sentences with a relative pronoun.

1 This is the table .... looks like an antique.

2 We first met in a town .... there are now several new shopping centres.

3 I met a man .... sister owns a chain of supermarkets.

4 It was Anita Roddick .... opened her first beauty shop in Brighton.

5 He's the jeweller .... necklaces have been seen in major fashion shows.

6 It is Harrods .... is the world-famous department store in London.

7 The man .... is talking to the shop assistant is my cousin.

8 We bought our little corner shop .... most people did their shopping locally.

I Read the pairs of sentences below. Use a relative pronoun to join them together and make any other necessary changes.

1 **a** The woman works at the jeweller's.
b The woman is French.

....

....

2 **a** This is the bookshop.
b I worked here last year.

....

....

3 **a** John will never forget the day.
b A fire destroyed his corner shop.

....

....

4 **a** They wanted to see the manager.
b Her sales figures were the best in the company.

....

....

5 **a** A bag holds a lot of shopping.
b A bag must be strong.

....

....

Speaking Link

J In pairs, ask and answer these questions.

- Do you like shopping?
- Do you ever shop late at night or order things from the Internet?
- What kinds of things do you enjoy buying, and what do you hate buying?
- Are there any shops in your country which are open 24 hours a day?
- If there aren't, do you think it would be a good idea to have shops which never close?

Writing Link

K In this unit you are going to learn how to write a letter of complaint. Read the question and the advertisement below.

Imagine that you have just bought a new mobile phone, which you had seen advertised in a local newspaper. You spent a long time deciding which one to buy and made your decision very carefully. Unfortunately, it is nothing like the one in the advertisement and it has a number of problems. Look carefully at the advertisement and the notes you have made. Write a letter to the company, explaining what is wrong with the phone and ask for a replacement or a refund.

HINTS

When you are writing a letter of complaint, you must make sure that you are polite. You probably feel very angry, but if you sound rude, the person you are complaining to is not going to be very helpful.

L Read the following sentences. Choose the most polite option **a** or **b**.

1 **a** I was very surprised to find that the telephone is neither small nor lightweight, as advertised.
b I was really annoyed when I saw the phone – it's huge and it weighs a ton!

2 **a** To make matters worse, the phone I received is black, which was not one of the colours advertised.
b Can't you even get the colour right?

3 **a** I didn't get the free adaptor and earphone. Why not?
b Unfortunately, I did not receive the adaptor and earphone as advertised. I would like to hear your explanation for this.

4 **a** What's the point of giving free things if they don't fit?
b I was very disappointed to find that the case is not the right size.

5 **a** In your advertisement you say that the mobile phone is easy to use, but I still have not found the main menu.
b You lied about the phone being easy to use – it's really difficult!

6 **a** You'd better give me a new phone, or my money back!
b Could you please make arrangements to refund my money or give me a new mobile phone?

M Now write your letter of complaint, using the polite sentences from task L above, and the outline below. (140-160 words)

Letter Outline	
Greeting	Dear Sir/Madam
Paragraph 1	Say why you are writing and give the basic details of what you are complaining about.
Paragraphs 2 and 3	Give details of what was advertised and what you actually received.
Closing paragraph	Tell the reader what action you expect him/her to take, and that you would appreciate a prompt reply.
Signing off	Yours faithfully (your name)

Unit 14 Food

A Look at the photographs of different places to eat and drink.
Have you ever been in any of these situations? Did you enjoy yourself?
Is there anywhere that you would NOT like to go?

B Where do you think the following people would most like to go?
Remember to give reasons for your answers.

1 a young couple celebrating their first wedding anniversary ☐	2 a group of friends spending the weekend together ☐	3 a family with two children going on holiday ☐

Reading Link

C Now read the article quickly to find three things which could spoil a picnic.

PICNIC FUN

PENNY SWEET **shares her experience of eating out in the open.**

Summer is just around the corner and it's possible that this time tomorrow you'll be sitting in the countryside having a picnic. Lucky you! But before you dig out your old picnic hamper or, even worse, buy a new one, here's a word of warning. Things are never quite as idyllic as they seem.

The whole idea of going on a picnic is that you have a great time eating outdoors. This takes rather a lot of things for granted. First of all, there's the food itself. If you have romantic ideas of chilled wine, pâté and fresh salads, then think again! Unless you take all the contents of your kitchen with you (corkscrews, glasses, salt and pepper, etc) or spend an absolute fortune on a picnic hamper, the chances are that you are not really going to enjoy your meal.

Secondly, choose your spot carefully. The only thing worse than spending hours looking for the best location, unpacking the car, arguing about where to put the travel blanket (Don't even think about beautifully clean white tablecloths – you will be trying to get rid of the grass stains for ages!) is realising that there is a bull in the same field as you! The next thing to remember is never to take fizzy drinks on a picnic.

> ‘Things are never quite as idyllic as they seem.’

If you have never run like the wind to escape a swarm of angry, sugar-starved wasps, you probably don't understand the logic behind this, but take it from someone who knows; it may sound funny to you, but it was anything but amusing at the time!

Wasps can, however, be kept away – at least far enough away so that you can eat your picnic in peace! Take an empty but unwashed jam jar and add a little water. Leave this some distance from the spot you have chosen for your picnic. Make sure that it is far enough away so that any wasps that are attracted to it do not bother you, but not so far away that they are more interested in your lunch than the jam jar!

Apart from the local wildlife, the weather can also help you to decide whether or not your picnic will be a success. In most parts of Britain, it's not so much a case of mad dogs and Englishmen going out in the midday sun as going out in a gale force wind!

So don't forget that great invention – only a Brit could have thought of this one – the windbreak. Rather like a sheet on poles, it is designed to protect picnickers and sunbathers from the wind, although the enjoyment factor is questionable. It's not much fun when there are four of you sitting almost on top of each other in a very small space just to avoid ending up with sandy sandwiches.

Is it really worth all the effort, you may ask? Well, I don't know about you, but I'll be having my meals in the comfort of my dining room this summer!

D Read the article again and answer the following questions.

1 According to the writer, what is necessary for a good picnic?
  a nice food and a clean tablecloth
  b spending lots of money on food
  c taking everything you need with you
  d taking wine with you

2 Which of the following is the worst thing that could happen on a picnic?
  a taking ages to unpack the car
  b quarrelling about where to sit
  c finding a good place to have a picnic
  d realising there is a bull in the field

3 What is the best thing to do if you don't want wasps to spoil your picnic?
  a Place a jam jar next to your picnic spot.
  b Make sure that the jam jar is far away from you.
  c Put a jam jar in some water.
  d Put a jam jar somewhere so that the wasps will leave your lunch alone.

4 Why is a windbreak useful on a picnic?
  a It can be very windy in Britain.
  b You can sunbathe.
  c It doesn't need much space.
  d You can sit close together.

5 What is the writer's opinion of picnics?
  a They should be avoided at all costs.
  b They can be enjoyable, but they need a lot of preparation.
  c They are a complete waste of time.
  d They are definitely worth the effort.

Vocabulary Link

E Match the words from the article with their meanings.

Words	Meanings
1 hamper	a something you use to open a bottle which has a cork
2 corkscrew	b a basket you use to put picnic things in
3 fortune	c animals and plants in nature
4 spot	d a dirty mark which does not go away when you wash it
5 location	e the place you have chosen
6 stain	f a lot of money
7 wildlife	g something which influences something else
8 factor	h a place where something happens

F Use the following phrases from the article to complete the sentences.

take (something) for granted — take it from someone who knows — anything but — get rid of — worth the effort

1 Don't believe the restaurant guide; I went to eat at the new Mexican place last night and the food was .... tasty.

2 Don't put a beautiful cloth on the table; it's not .... Jane's children always make a mess when they are eating.

3 Some teenagers .... it .... that their mothers will always cook their meals for them.

4 I really think you should .... all that mess in the kitchen before your mother gets home.

5 ....: never ask your husband to go to the delicatessen for you because he will always spend more than you had planned.

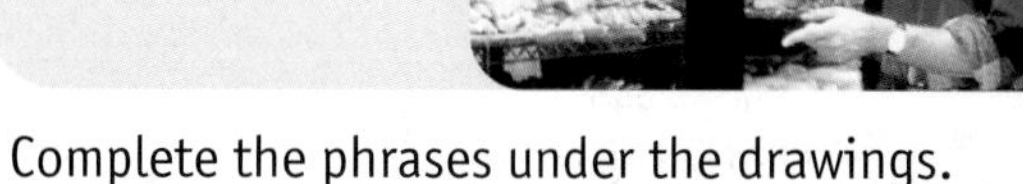

G Complete the phrases under the drawings.

a bag of — a bottle of — a box of — a bunch of — a cube of — a tin of — a jar of — a packet of — a sack of

1 .... grapes

2 .... sugar

3 .... chocolates

4 .... biscuits

5 .... peas

6 .... flour

7 .... jam

8 .... water

9 .... crisps

Grammar Link

Future Continuous

Read this sentence taken from the article.

... *it's possible that this time tomorrow you**'ll be sitting** in the countryside having a picnic.*

Which tense in this sentence is used to talk about an action that will be in progress at a specific time in the future?

....

Complete the following rule.

The .... tense is used to talk about an action which will be in progress at a specific .... in the future.

Study the Grammar Reference on page 109 before you do to the tasks.

H Use the verbs below in the Future Continuous tense to complete the sentences which follow.

work go wait drink discuss

1 I .... to the butcher's later. Do you want any lamb chops?

2 Don't ring me between six and seven o'clock. I .... the menu with the chef then.

3 I can't help you to prepare for the party because I .... tomorrow.

4 This time next week we .... our homemade wine.

5 Don't be late because I .... for you outside the restaurant.

I Complete the sentences with the correct form of the verb given, using either the Future Simple or the Future Continuous.

1 If I'm lucky, this time tomorrow evening I .... (have) dinner in the new restaurant.

2 They .... (not/eat) breakfast at 6 am next week when they're on holiday.

3 Do you think you .... (try) some fried seaweed when you arrive in Japan tomorrow morning?

4 Don't worry about washing the dishes! I .... (do) them later.

5 If you're going to the supermarket, ... (you/get) me some eggs so I can make a soufflé for dinner?

6 .... (your husband/cook) for your son when you go into hospital next week?

Speaking Link

J Look at the photographs showing different kinds of food. Compare and contrast the photographs, saying which kind of food you prefer.

A

healthy, variety, salads, crisp vegetables, pasta, lettuce, onions, peppers

B

unhealthy, junk food, chips, tomato sauce, hamburger, soft drinks, sweets, cakes, crisps

- Which kind of food shown in the photographs is more popular with teenagers in your country?
- Why do you think this is?

Writing Link

In this unit, you will learn how to write an article.

K Look at the question and put the article in the correct order.

Imagine that the editor of your school newspaper has asked you to write an article about the worst meal you have ever had. Write your article describing where you had the meal, and the meal itself.

The Worst Meal I've Ever Had

A

You'll never guess what happened next! The waiters brought us the wrong food, saying that the chefs had got the orders mixed up! **But the worst was yet to come!** The food was awful, but when we complained, the waiter told us no one else had complained, so it was too bad!

B

We were so angry that we paid the bill and left, without leaving a tip, of course! I won't count on anyone's reputation again, and I advise you to do the same!

C

Have you heard the expression 'Too many cooks spoil the broth'? Well, I discovered how true it is at the most popular restaurant in town.

D

I have never seen anything so chaotic in my life! There were more staff than customers, and waiters were running about all over the place. **To make matters even worse,** it took ages to get our food because the chefs were never in the kitchen; they were telling jokes and talking to the customers.

Paragraph 1	☐	Paragraph 3	☐
Paragraph 2	☐	Paragraph 4	☐

L Why has the writer used the phrases and sentences in bold? ....
....
....
....
....

M Now write your own article, using the outline below and some of the phrases from the article opposite. (140-160 words)

Article Outline

Paragraph 1	Introduce the article in an interesting way, perhaps with a question or a joke.
Paragraphs 2 and 3	Give details of the meal, using logical paragraphs. Do your best to keep the reader interested.
Paragraph 4	Say how the meal ended and what you have learnt from it. You could also give some advice on how to avoid such a situation.

HINTS

When you write an article, think about your reader. Here, you are writing for people who are the same age as you and who probably have the same interests as you. Write as if you are speaking directly to them, not down to them. You must also try to keep them interested. In this particular question, it would be good if you could make it funny – and don't forget to use your imagination!

Listening Link

N Listen to part of a seminar on vegetarian cooking and complete the student's notebook.

Points to remember when cooking vegetarian food

1. Vegetables should be cooked quickly because it helps to ....
2. .... and .... are cooked first when making a Chinese stir-fry.
3. Salads shouldn't be prepared ....
4. Most people prefer food that ....
5. Children can take .... to school.
6. At least .... % of your diet should contain raw food every day.
7. Many teenagers are overweight because they eat ....
8. Vegetarian food is healthy and ....

Unit 15 Education

A Work in small groups and do a survey to see how many hours students in your class spend doing their homework. You can make a chart to show how many hours are spent every day, every week or every month for each of the different subjects you study at school.

Reading Link

B Read quickly through the article below and the missing paragraphs opposite and then work with a partner to make a summary of the main arguments for and against having homework.

Austria 50 Sch
Belgium 110 Fr
Canada $4·25
Canary Isles 400 Ptas
Cyprus £1·50
Denmark 21·50 Kr
Finland 30 FM
France 16 Fr
Germany 5·10 DM
Gibraltar £1·25
Greece 850 Drs
Holland 6·35 Fl

The Evenin

* * *

No. 40,102

Your Quality Newspa

Have You Finished Your Homework?

By the time you read this article, you will probably have done about 18 months' homework in your school life!

When I was a child, homework was the cause of many arguments between my parents. My mother believed that homework was the only way for us to make progress. My father, on the other hand, thought we should have learnt everything we needed to know while we were in school.

1

It is true to say, though, that most students don't want to know anything about homework. In this age of leisure, it seems inhuman to expect our young people to do four or five hours of homework while their parents are watching television. We know that by the time they finish their homework, they will have missed all the interesting programmes.

As a result of recent research, many experts believe that homework is a complete waste of time, especially when many children appear to get their homework done by someone else. In fact, some people say that the only positive result of giving homework is that children become very creative in finding new excuses for not having done it.

Apart from parents and people in education, there are other people who suggest that school should be like a modern business. Most good managers do not take their work home, but manage their time and complete their work during their working hours.

Personally, I think that a simple change in the timetable at school would allow children to do individual work with a teacher around to help, if needed. Teachers wouldn't feel so tired as there would be less marking and students would have a better balance between study and rest times.

C Now see if you can put the missing paragraphs in the correct place in the article. There is an extra paragraph which you don't need to use.

A
Other professionals would disagree, saying that it is good for education to be continued at home and for parents to be involved. They think that it is good for children to work alone and to try to practise what they are supposed to have learnt in class.

B
So, why can't children and teachers do the same? Imagine a life without homework. You would need fewer books and you would spend less energy on moving the millions of books from one place to another. Not only that, a lot of time would be saved.

C
Homework gives both teachers and students a headache. By next September, I will have been teaching at the same school for 19 years. I have seen that the teacher has two types of problem. Firstly, to make sure that the homework is done and in a way that is readable. Secondly, teachers continue to make complaints about the number of books they have to carry from school to home and back again.

D
I have to admit my mother was right. When you didn't do your homework, you were the first to suffer. Teachers found ways of making you feel silly in front of your classmates, and parents even tried to stop their children's pocket money.

E
Don't think that parents like the idea of homework, either! They don't. In our fast-moving world, most parents are now faced with the problem of not being able to understand what their children are learning. These parents prefer to listen to modern opinion that says leave the homework at school.

F
Unfortunately, as the world becomes more and more competitive, it seems that homework is here to stay. Perhaps future students will find a way to get their computers to do their homework for them!

Vocabulary Link

D Read these examples from the article with **make** and **do**.

*... the only way for us to **make** progress ...*
*... allow children to **do** individual work ...*

Now look at the table and study the other phrases with **make** and **do**. Then, complete the table with these words.

an excuse certain damage wrong **a complaint** work

Make	Do
an attempt	one's best
an arrangement	business (with)
a decision	a course
a difference	a favour
an effort	good
fun of	harm
a mistake	homework
money	research
a profit	the shopping
progress	well
....	....
....	....
....	....

E Complete the sentences below by using **make** or **do** in the correct form.

1 I think he .... a lot of progress when he gets a new teacher.
2 Don't worry! I .... that favour for you. I promise.
3 I only .... one mistake in the last test.
4 As long as you .... your best, I will be happy.
5 Take the medicine. It .... you good.
6 Computers .... a difference to teaching methods since they were introduced into schools.

F Match the phrasal verbs with their meanings.

1 **hurry up**

2 **cross out**

3 **go on**

4 **tidy up**

- **a** make neat and clean
- **b** continue
- **c** give to a specific person
- **d** move quickly
- **e** give to a number of people
- **f** erase
- **g** put a line through

5 **rub out**

6 **give in**

7 **give out**

G Put the phrasal verbs above into the sentences in their correct form.

1 The teacher wasn't very happy when the students forgot .... the classroom.

2 Maria can't .... like this all year! She studies all night and never sleeps.

3 Student demonstrators .... leaflets yesterday morning in protest against the new exam system.

4 John didn't .... any homework last term, so the teacher decided to send him to the head teacher.

5 When Penny .... her wrong answers, she almost makes a hole in her paper.

6 Unless they .... , they are not going to get to school on time.

7 The exercise will be easier if you .... the words as you use them.

Grammar Link

Future Perfect Simple, Future Perfect Continuous

Read these sentences from the article and the missing paragraphs. Which tenses are used? ....
....

By the time you read this article, you ***will*** *probably* ***have done*** *about 18 months' homework in your school life!*

By next September, I ***will have been teaching*** *at the same school for 19 years.*

Complete the following rules.

The .... tense is used to talk about something that will have happened before a certain time in the ....
The .... tense is used to talk about how long something will have been in progress at a certain time in the future.

Study the Grammar Reference on pages 109 and 110 before you do the task.

H Complete the following sentences by putting the verbs in brackets into the Future Perfect Simple or Future Perfect Continuous.

1 By the time we get to the lesson, it .... (start).

2 .... (you / finish) your homework before your father gets home?

3 By the end of the year, the head teacher .... (work) in this school for 15 years.

4 She .... (forget) all the things you have taught her in a few years' time.

5 I .... (do) all my homework by the time the match starts.

6 I .... (complete) the project by the end of this term.

7 When my sister leaves university, she .... (study) for 18 years!

8 I am sure our teacher .... (not / forget) to mark our tests.

Listening Link 

I You will hear four teachers talking to students about job opportunities. For questions 1-4, choose from the list (**a-e**) to show which qualifications each student will need. There is one extra letter which you do not need to use.

a a degree in languages
b work experience
c a secretarial diploma
d a certificate of attendance
e a school-leaving certificate

Dialogue 1  Dialogue 3 
Dialogue 2  Dialogue 4

Speaking Link 

J Work with a partner and talk about the qualities of an ideal teacher. Choose the three most important qualities from the list below. Put them in order starting with the quality you think is the most important. It doesn't matter if you don't agree with each other, but you must give reasons for your opinions.

- good sense of humour
- ability to keep control
- excellent knowledge of the subject
- patience
- ability to express yourself
- ability to relate to young people

I think we should include ... because ... .
The obvious choice is ..., because ... .
Do you think ... is more important than ...?
I don't agree. I think it's very important that a teacher is ... .
Do you think we should put ... first/next/after ...?

Now report back to the class.

Writing Link 

You have already looked at one kind of story in Unit 5. In this unit, you are going to write a story that begins or ends with specific words.

Don't forget the five things that make a good story! (See Unit 5)

K Read the question and the story below, and fill the gaps with the correct form of the verb in brackets.

Your teacher has asked your class to write stories beginning or ending with the following words: ***I couldn't believe my luck; this was the chance of a lifetime!***

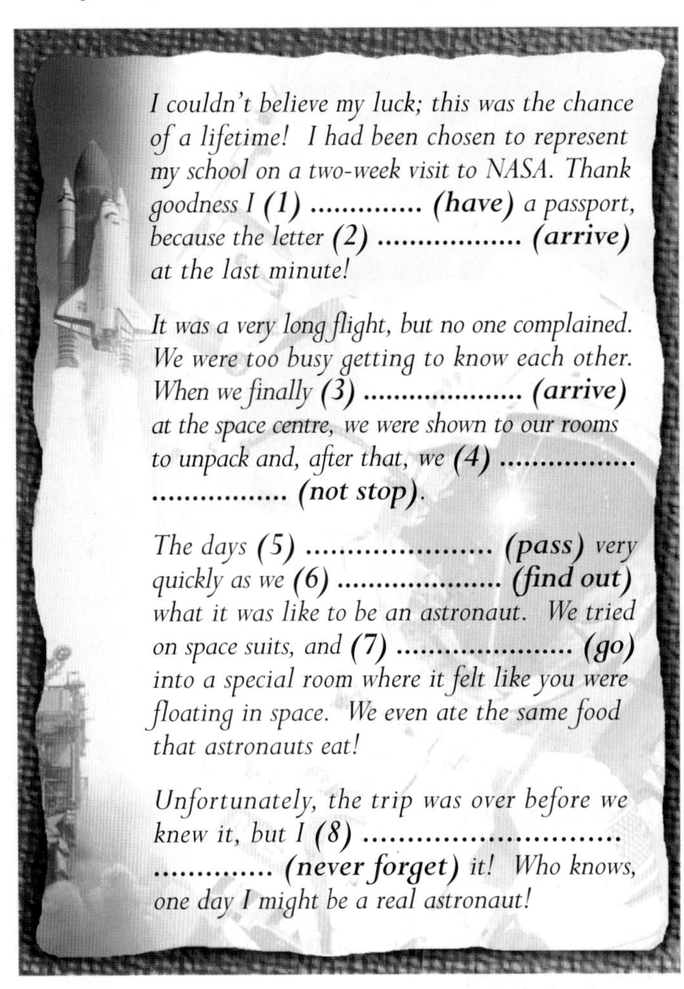

I couldn't believe my luck; this was the chance of a lifetime! I had been chosen to represent my school on a two-week visit to NASA. Thank goodness I ***(1)*** .... ***(have)*** *a passport, because the letter* ***(2)*** .... ***(arrive)*** *at the last minute!*

It was a very long flight, but no one complained. We were too busy getting to know each other. When we finally ***(3)*** .... ***(arrive)*** *at the space centre, we were shown to our rooms to unpack and, after that, we* ***(4)*** .... ***(not stop)****.*

The days ***(5)*** .... ***(pass)*** *very quickly as we* ***(6)*** .... ***(find out)*** *what it was like to be an astronaut. We tried on space suits, and* ***(7)*** .... ***(go)*** *into a special room where it felt like you were floating in space. We even ate the same food that astronauts eat!*

Unfortunately, the trip was over before we knew it, but I ***(8)*** .... ***(never forget)*** *it! Who knows, one day I might be a real astronaut!*

L Read the outline below and then write your own story. (140-160 words)

Story Outline

Paragraph 1	Introduce your story by setting the scene. (Begin with the words given.)
Paragraph 2	Continue your story up to the climax.
Paragraph 3	Describe the climax.
Paragraph 4	Say what happened as a result of the event. (End with the words given.)

HINTS

- You must make sure that you understand exactly what the words mean. If you don't understand, your whole story will be wrong!
- You cannot change the words given, so you must think carefully about how to link your ideas.

Unit 16 Technology

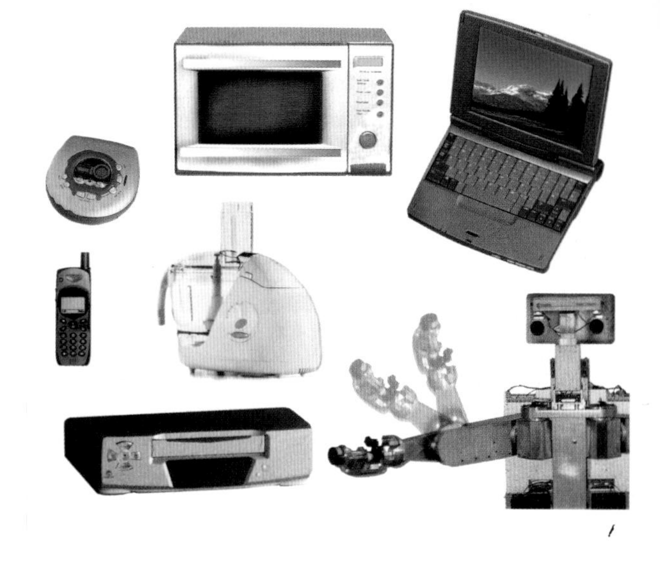

A How many of these items have you got at home?

B Now work with a friend and decide which of the items you could NOT live without. Give reasons for your choice.

Reading Link

C Look at the advertisements. Say which one you would choose to buy or use and explain why this item or service would help you to improve your life.

teenscape hi-tech shopping

A

Change your Image

*A fast, reliable service is provided for the young man or woman who wants to make an impression. **CompuBeauty** uses the latest technology to help you change your whole life painlessly and inexpensively!*

***CompuBeauty** uses computer imaging techniques to let you see which hairstyle is right for you. Experiment with make up to see what colours suit you. 'Try on' different styles of clothing to see how you could look, without paying for expensive mistakes.*

For a one-hour appointment with one of our experts you will get

- *personal and professional attention.*
- *computer printouts of your final choices.*
- *special discounts on all hair and beauty products.*
- *vouchers giving you 15% discount on all clothes in any of our **CompuBeauty** shops.*

Just bring two recent photos – a close-up shot of your face and a full-length one.

Special offer until the end of the month: only £50!!

Phone us on 020-9846002 immediately for an appointment.

B

Personal Robot

Make your parents and teachers happy!

Are you having problems finishing your homework on time? Do you avoid tidying your room until your mum shouts at you? You don't need to worry if you buy a Mr Helping Hand personal robot. Mr H can be programmed to organise your homework and can help you do the work faster. Your own personal robot will follow you around, putting away books and objects that are left lying on the floor or bed.

Mr H has also got the following features:

- *>> weighs only 3 kgs*
- *>> long life batteries*
- *>> a 5-year guarantee*
- *>> remembers simple instructions*

Originally sold for £229
NOW ONLY £150

You can buy your personal robot from all branches of Spark Electrics.

C

This is a watch that James Bond would be proud to wear! This is NOT a watch for ordinary people!

Your electronic *PENGO WATCH CONTROL*

* acts as a remote control for TVs and videos.
* sets off a silent warning alarm when parents or teachers are near.
* gives you a daily weather forecast.
* reminds you when to hand in your homework.

This amazing electronic watch has also got a security code lock.

In addition to all this, your *PENGO WATCH CONTROL* will always tell you the time accurately!

Special introductory price of £61.99 including a 5-year guarantee. Order before 1st March and you will be sent two free tickets to the latest James Bond film showing at your nearest cinema.

Details on 0800-641853

D

Using the latest technology, our new lightweight clothes come with the following features:

- *automatic repair of any tears or holes*
- *one size to fit everybody (material adjusts to all sizes)*
- *smart colour changes (up to four choices) when you press the electronic chip built into the label*
- *material adapts to outside and body temperatures to provide maximum comfort*

WEAR and TEAR's clothes don't need ironing – so Mums will like them, too.

Available only by mail order. Deliveries guaranteed within three days of receiving orders. Prices include p & p.

Telephone for catalogue: 0921-684848 (24-hour customer service).

E

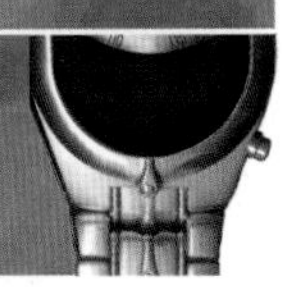

This cool bike is guaranteed to make your friends green with envy!

SUPABYKE electronic is an amazing product using the latest technology for bikes and cars. Made from super lightweight material it weighs only 2 kgs!! Not only that, it folds up to a size that will fit in the average school bag. Just imagine riding to school, getting off your bike, folding it up and putting it into your bag. Your friends will be amazed!

SUPABYKE's intelligent power system will help you cycle up hills without getting out of breath. The easy-to-use software guarantees that you will never get lost. SUPABYKE has a built-in homing device that will allow you to get back home safely from wherever you are.

Available in flashy red, sporty green and electric blue.

Special price of £999.99 includes carrying cover and smart accessories.

Come and inspect the bike and go for a test ride at our main shop in Wolton High Street.

D Answer the following questions by reading through the advertisements. Be prepared to give reasons for your answers.

Which item(s) would be bought or used by

somebody travelling in different climates?	1	
a person who wants to know when grown-ups are nearby?	2	
somebody who doesn't want to get tired?	3	4
a person interested in looking good?	5	
a forgetful person?	6	
somebody who doesn't have to worry about money?	7	8
a person who wants to try the product before buying?	9	

Now choose the best answer to the following question.

10 Where would you be most likely to find these advertisements?

- **a** in a science magazine
- **b** in a company brochure
- **c** in a magazine for young people
- **d** in a Sunday newspaper

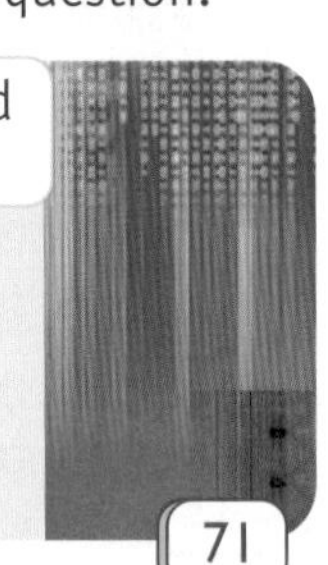

Vocabulary Link

E The words and phrases below have been taken from the advertisments. Circle the word or phrase closest in meaning to each one.

1	appointment (advert A)	a a job b an arrangement to meet
2	features (advert B)	a important parts of something b parts of somebody's face
3	guarantee (advert B)	a safety b a promise
4	remote (advert C)	a from a distance b switch
5	accurately (advert C)	a without any mistakes b cleanly
6	catalogue (advert D)	a list b small book
7	latest (advert E)	a most recent b last
8	average (advert E)	a usual b result

F Complete the sentences with a form of the words in capitals. All the words are in the adverts.

1. Scientists agreed that the results of the first tests were not .... and so they decided to do them again. ***RELY***
2. The remote-controlled spaceship made an .... on toy manufacturers. ***IMPRESS***
3. Have you heard the .... news about the Russian space station? ***LATE***
4. She was able to walk quickly and .... with the help of the new injections. ***PAIN***
5. Researchers have found a way of testing new cosmetics .... without using animals. ***EXPENSIVE***
6. Out of all the science subjects at school, Terry's .... favourite was biology. ***PERSON***
7. The court said that the inventor's behaviour had not been very .... and it asked for a public apology. ***PROFESSION***
8. Unfortunately, when it comes to being used in experiments, animals don't have any .... in the matter. ***CHOOSE***
9. The chemist told the woman that the medicine would work .... if she rested. ***FAST***
10. Before you use the chemicals in this box, please read all the .... ***INSTRUCT***

Grammar Link

Gerund and Infinitive

Read the following parts of sentences taken from the adverts.

*Do you **avoid tidying** your room ...?*
*Just **imagine riding** to school ...*

Which form of the verb follows the verbs **avoid** and **imagine**? ....

See 16.1 of the Grammar Reference on page 110 for a list of verbs that are followed by the gerund.

Read the following parts of sentences taken from the adverts.

*... for the young man or woman who **wants to make** an impression.*
*You **don't need to worry** ...*

Which form of the verb follows the verbs **want** and **need**? ....

See 16.2 of the Grammar Reference on page 110 for a list of verbs that are followed by the full infinitive.

G Complete the following sentences by putting the verbs in brackets into the correct form.

1. Have you ever thought about .... (get) a DVD system?
2. I wouldn't risk .... (keep) my discs in an unlocked drawer.
3. They managed .... (find out) where the computer virus had come from.
4. He couldn't imagine her .... (study) biology at university.
5. I don't enjoy .... (do) dangerous experiments in the laboratory.
6. Do they allow you .... (use) the computers whenever you want?
7. Can't you offer .... (lend) him your new video camera?
8. They started the research without .... (have) enough money to complete it.
9. We look forward to .... (see) you at the science fair.

Listening Link

H You will hear part of a discussion on radio about how much we depend on technology in our daily lives. Answer questions 1-6 by writing **P** for presenter, **F** for Fiona or **N** for neither.

1. Who feels that machines are taking over her life?

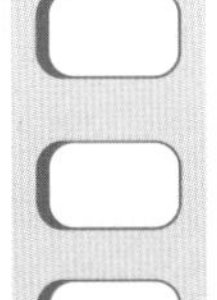
2. Who blames her husband for making life difficult?

3. Who apologises for being dependent on technology?

4. Who believes that we are not really making progress?
5. Who wants manufacturers to warn us about possible health risks?
6. Who thinks that women would be better designers of household equipment?

Speaking Link

I Work with a partner. Discuss these questions.

- Why do some people feel afraid of new technology, such as computers?
- How can computers help people?
- Do computers have any disadvantages?
- Do computers make people lazy?
- What do you think will be the next great development in technology?

Now report back to the class.

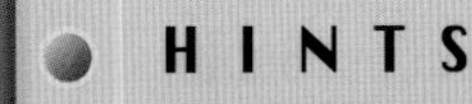

HINTS

If you read magazines or newspapers in English, you will learn more vocabulary that you can use when you are speaking.

Writing Link

In this unit, you are going to learn how to write a report. A report is usually written by someone who knows a lot about the subject and who has a particular reader in mind. Reports are written for different reasons and in this unit you are going to see how to write a report that gives suggestions or makes recommendations.

J Look at the question and the report and fill the gaps with the correct word or phrase from the box.

Imagine that your teacher is planning to ask the head teacher to buy some computers for the school. She has asked your class to write a report for the head teacher, giving suggestions on how computers could be used in the classroom. Write your report.

a Conclusion	**e** Introduction
b Date	**f** Projects and Presentations
c From	**g** Subject
d Information	**h** To

(1) .... : Mr Griffiths
(2) .... : James Harper
(3) .... : 30 October, 2002
(4) .... : Computers in the classroom

The Use of Computers in the Classroom

(5) ....

The purpose of this report is to make suggestions about how computers could be used in the classroom.

(6) ....

- An up-to-date encyclopaedia on CD could be used instead of the one available in the school library, which is out of date.
- Students could do research for school projects on the Internet. In this way, they would have all the latest information at their fingertips.

(7) ....

- Students could use computers to prepare homework and projects. This would enable them to design charts and diagrams, as well as to present their work in a professional way.

(8) ....

To sum up, it is obvious that computers have many uses in the classroom. In my opinion, our school would benefit greatly from having computers.

K Now write your own report, using the outline below. Don't forget to use headings! (140-160 words)

Report Outline

Heading	Think of a suitable title for your report.
Paragraph 1	Say what you are going to talk about in your report.
Paragraphs 2 and 3	Make your points and your suggestions or recommendations.
Paragraph 4	Make a final comment on your suggestions or recommendations.

Review 4 Units 13 14 15 16

A Complete the following article by choosing **a**, **b** or **c**.

Happy Shopping

Many parents nowadays are asking whether it is **(1)** .... the effort to take their teenage children shopping. Why waste hours walking from one shop to another when you can **(2)** .... all your shopping on the Internet? In addition, teenagers are usually anything **(3)** .... practical or cost conscious!

I remember years ago when my mother would take the whole family out shopping at the beginning of September. We were allowed one new **(4)** .... of shoes each. These shoes, **(5)** .... design and cost caused many arguments, were supposed to last for the whole winter. If the shops we visited thought they were going to **(6)** .... a profit from my mother, then they were wrong. She avoided **(7)** .... more than necessary and insisted **(8)** .... getting a guarantee that the shoes were waterproof.

Today, of course, shopping **(9)** .... have changed. Just when you think you will **(10)** .... saving money at the local shop, your sons and daughters are sure to be spending more on the Internet. They are the ones who will **(11)** .... been using your credit cards and they will **(12)** .... to know why you are changing your bank account! No doubt the time will come **(13)** .... they have their own children and will understand what the problem was. However, in the meantime, you should always be careful **(14)** .... you hide your purse.

	a	b	c	d
1	value	cost	ⓒ worth	make
2	make	do	have	put
3	other	else	above	but
4	couple	pair	few	box
5	who	which	whose	their
6	have	make	do	take
7	to pay	having paid	paying	being paid
8	on	to	for	with
9	hobbies	customs	habits	ways
10	to be	be	have been	can
11	can	having	have	to go
12	wanting	to want	want	wanted
13	which	that	where	when
14	where	how	which	whose

B Rewrite the second sentence so that it has a similar meaning to the first one. Use the word in bold to rewrite the sentence. The first one has been done for you.

1 Penny has managed to win a scholarship to her local university.
succeeded
Penny has ....*succeeded in winning*.... a scholarship to her local university.

2 My mother never let me eat in front of the television.
allowed
My mother .... in front of the television.

3 Mrs Wade left the store but she forgot to pay for a scarf she'd picked up.
without
Mrs Wade left the store .... for a scarf she'd picked up.

4 I won't have any more experiments to do after Wednesday.
done
I .... all my experiments by Wednesday.

5 I've booked a table so that I can have dinner with Emma on Friday.
will
Emma and I .... dinner together on Friday.

C Circle the word that completes the sentences correctly.

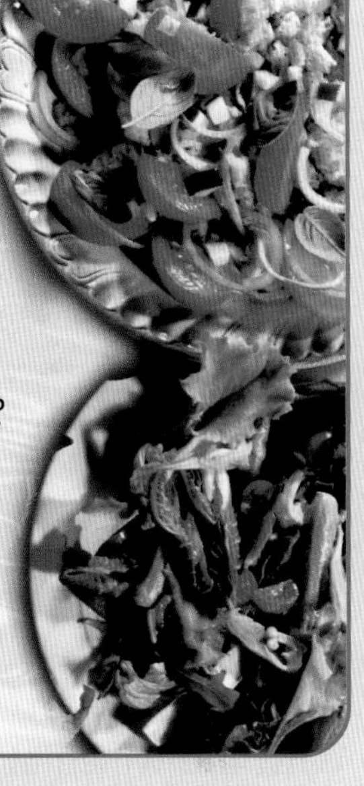

1 Have you **done / made** a mistake in this maths problem?

2 He avoided **spending / to spend** too much by leaving his credit card at home.

3 They will **be building / have built** the new shopping centre by the end of next year.

4 I'm looking forward to **go / going** back to school.

5 I actually studied with the professor **which / who** wrote that book.

6 Would you mind **to buy / buying** some fish for me.

7 Can you imagine **to become / becoming** famous by making an important scientific discovery?

8 The teachers will **be having / have** a meeting tomorrow afternoon.

9 Several scientists have attempted **to discover / discovering** how to cure the common cold, but they have not succeeded so far.

10 I'll **do / make** an effort to get the meal ready on time.

D Put the phrasal verbs in the sentences in their correct form.

cross out **give in** **give out** **hurry up** **rub out** **tidy up**

1 If you don't ....hurry up..... and fill in the form, you won't be able to go to university this year.

2 When I go shopping, I .... the things on my shopping list after I have put them in my basket.

3 The teacher told them to .... the library before the next class came in.

4 The pupils .... their suggestions for what they wanted to eat at the end-of-term party.

5 The Institute of Technology .... leaflets all day next Thursday to advertise their new computer courses.

6 When George saw the teacher coming, he quickly .... the cartoons he had drawn on the board.

E Match the parts of sentences.

1 Most shops try to take
2 When you go into a first-class restaurant, you take it
3 I'm going to get
4 He used a laser pen to draw the bunch
5 If you make
6 It's not possible to do

a rid of my old computer and buy a laptop.
b your shopping in less than an hour on Friday nights.
c of grapes for the new advertisement.
d advantage of you during the sales.
e for granted that the food will be good.
f a mistake on the till, just ring for the supervisor.

Unit 17 Crime

A Match the verbs with the nouns to form phrases connected with crime. Use a dictionary to find the meaning of any unknown words.

1	commit	the law	a
2	rob	a watch	b
3	burgle	a crime	c
4	steal	a criminal	d
5	break	a bank	e
6	arrest	a house	f

Reading Link

B Read the article through quickly and say what jobs the three people do to earn money.

Does Crime Pay?

Crime correspondent Jane Wright recently interviewed three people whose contact with the world of crime is quite unusual.

1

As most of you must know, the fictional character James Bond has a licence to kill. He is a hero who travels around the world in order to fight the enemies of his government. His adventures, of course, are fictional. However, there are people who have a real licence to kill and others who kill, believing they are right to do so.

2

Charlie B, 51, works at a top security prison, where prisoners who have been sentenced to death for murder wait to be executed. Up to now, he must have executed more than 25 prisoners. According to Charlie, the prisoners don't ask for a last meal or talk to their executioners. 'Their minds are no longer working normally. What am I going to say to them, anyway? "Hello, how are you?"'

3

So what does Charlie think of his job? Firstly, he is quick to point out that he never looks forward to an execution. He also says that, although he might feel sorry for the prisoners, he believes they deserve their punishment. 'They knew what the result of committing their crime would be,' he says. 'I am only doing what the law tells me to. My conscience is clear.'

4

Someone else who feels that his conscience is clear is John V, a 36-year-old policeman who has shot and killed twelve people while working. 'When I fire my gun it's because my life is threatened. It's either my life or someone else's,' he says. John honestly believes that he has only fired a shot when his life was in danger.

5

Unlike Charlie, the policeman is in danger every day. 'On one occasion we stopped a van which was being driven at high speed. As I got closer to it, the three passengers started shooting and I fell to the ground,' he remembers. Fortunately for him, they can't have realised he was still alive, because they stopped shooting at him and concentrated on the other police officers. While they were doing this, he managed to kill two of them.

6

One person who is not paid to kill legally is a man who calls himself Simon E. Simon, an ex-soldier, is hired to kill, but he is not like the hired men seen in films. He says that he will only shoot people he thinks are evil. 'When I read about the person, and I see that they couldn't have lived a good life, I feel that I am just helping society,' he explains.

7

Most of us don't like violence, so you might have been surprised to read that some people are, in fact, paid to kill. We can't blame these people for their behaviour, because we don't know what we might do in the same situation. Research has shown that there is often a fine line between what we think is right or wrong. We could do something that we believe is right and that others think is a crime. Each situation must be judged separately.

C Now read the article again and match the following summary sentences with parts 1-7.

A There are people who believe they are doing others a favour. [ ]

B It is not necessary to feel bad about the job because you are doing what you are told to do. [ ]

C Sometimes you have to kill in order to protect yourself. [ ]

D Some things that happen in stories, happen in real life, too. [ ]

E It is not easy to decide where justice stops and crime begins. [ ]

F The punishment is similar to the crime. [ ]

G Every day there is a risk of dying while you are doing your job. [ ]

Vocabulary Link

D The words and phrases below have been taken from the article and the summary sentences. Circle the word or phrase closest in meaning to each one.

1 fictional (part 1)	a stupid	b imaginary
2 licence (part 1)	a permission	b weapon
3 sentenced (part 2)	a told	b given punishment
4 point out (part 3)	a bring your attention to	b say something sharply
5 conscience (part 4)	a knowing right from wrong	b feeling all your senses
6 managed (part 5)	a tried	b succeeded
7 evil (part 6)	a very bad	b stupid
8 justice (summary sentences)	a excuse	b right behaviour

E Match the words below and join them with **and** or **or** to make new phrases.

alive, clean, hit, law, now, right, safe, sooner

later, order, run, sound, then, tidy, well, wrong

1 ....

2 ....

3 ....

4 ....

5 ....

6 ....

7 ....

8 ....

F Now put the phrases from Task E in the sentences below.

1 Many children don't learn the difference between what is .... because they are not given a good example by the adults around them.

2 Every .... we hear a burglar alarm and we know that somebody has tried to break into the bank again.

3 The young girl was found .... after being left in the woods by her kidnappers.

4 Researchers say that nobody can avoid crime – .... in your lifetime your house will be burgled.

5 The old lady went to bed feeling .... after her son had fitted new locks on her front door.

6 The little boy was taken to hospital with a broken leg after being knocked down by a .... driver.

7 Penny had left her house .... and was shocked when she returned home after her holiday to find a big mess left by burglars.

8 The judge said that when there was no .... on the streets, the crime figures increased.

Grammar Link

Modals – Possibility and Certainty

Read these examples from the article.

*... although he **might** feel sorry for the prisoners ...*
*We **could** do something that we believe is right ...*

Do the modals **might** and **could** refer to something that is certain or something that is possible?

....

Which form of the verb follows the modal?

....

Now, look at these examples.

*As most of you **must** know, ...*
*We **can't** blame these people for their behaviour, ...*

Do the modals **must** and **can't** refer to something that is certain, or something that is possible?

....

What period of time do these sentences refer to?

....

Complete the following rule.

We use the modals .... and **could** for situations that are .... and we use the modals .... and **can't** for situations that are ....

Study the Grammar Reference on page 111 before you do the tasks.

G Complete the sentences below by choosing the correct alternatives.

1 She **can't see / can't have seen** what happened because she wasn't there.

2 I'm not sure why he went home. He **couldn't have forgotten / might have forgotten** some important papers for the court case.

3 Our lawyer isn't here yet. He **must be / can't not be** on his way.

4 He **mustn't be / can't be** guilty. He was at home when the robbery took place.

5 He **must have stolen / must steal** the money when I went to answer the phone.

H Complete the second sentence so that it means the same as the first one, using the word given.

1 I'm sure he has a good lawyer because he is never convicted.
must
He .... a good lawyer because he is never convicted.

2 It's possible that Maggie took the money from the till.
might
Maggie .... the money from the till.

3 I'm absolutely sure she's not guilty because she'd never hurt anyone.
be
She .... guilty because she'd never hurt anyone.

4 I know for certain that Lee sent that threatening letter to the boss.
must
Lee .... that threatening letter to the boss.

5 It's possible that they didn't hear what you said about the burglary.
might
They .... what you said about the burglary.

6 It's possible that Paul knows why he was arrested.
might
Paul .... why he was arrested.

Speaking Link

I In pairs, ask and answer these questions. Use the words and expressions to help you.

- Have you ever done anything that you were punished for?
- What was your punishment? Did you deserve it?
- Have you ever done anything that you got away with? How did you feel?
- Has anyone punished you for something that you didn't do?
- How do you feel when you have done something that you know is wrong?
- What do you do to make yourself feel better?
- Do you make excuses for yourself?

harsh, guilty, unfair, detention, be grounded, be suspended from school

Listening Link

J Listen to people speaking in different situations. Choose which answer is correct from **a**, **b** or **c**.

1 Listen to this man speaking and decide who you think he is.
  a a burglar
  b a police officer
  c a witness

2 Listen to this woman talking. She is describing a man who
  a attacked her.
  b rescued her.
  c was knocked down.

3 You are listening to a report about crime. What is the biggest crime in most cities?
  a car theft
  b handbag snatching
  c drunken driving

4 Listen to a woman phoning a police station. What is the reason for her call?
  a Her car has been stolen.
  b Her cat is stuck in a tree.
  c She is locked out of her house.

5 You switch on the radio. What happened in the town centre this morning?
  a Somebody set fire to the health food shop.
  b A man attacked three school children.
  c A woman had £1,000 stolen from her bag.

6 You are in the bank when you hear this conversation. How did the customer behave?
  a She hit the robber over the head with her bag.
  b She screamed so loudly that the robber ran away.
  c She made the cashier finish serving her.

7 You will hear a policeman giving instructions about how to reach the court. How many times does the man have to turn left?
  a three times
  b once
  c not at all

8 Listen to this report from a policewoman. Who made the mistake?
  a the policewoman
  b the driver of the van
  c the driver of the car

Writing Link

In Unit 14, you learnt how to write an article of general interest. In this unit, you are going to learn to write an article that offers suggestions or solutions. As with all articles, it is very important that you think about the readers, so that you know what kind of suggestions or solutions to give.

K Look at the question below.

Imagine that you are a student representative of your school, and the head teacher has asked you to write an article for a magazine (published by a centre for teenagers who have broken the law), suggesting ways for young people to 'get back on the right track'. You should give realistic and practical suggestions for young people who have been in trouble with the police but want to make a new start.

L Complete the table with the words below.

because of, due to, for example, for instance, like, owing to, since, such as

Giving examples	Giving reasons
....	....
....	....
....	....
....	....

M Complete the following sentences using words from the table above. There may be more than one possible answer.

1 Go to places where you will be able to make new friends, ... youth clubs and sports centres.

2 .... you want to make an effort, you shouldn't have too many difficulties.

3 Make up for lost time at school. ...., you could go to night school to catch up with your education.

4 Do something for the community, ... helping people in need. It really is worth it!

5 Try to put your past behind you. You can't ruin your whole life .... what happened.

6 It may be difficult to find a job, ... the fact that you have been in trouble with the police, but lots of people are willing to give young people a second chance.

N Now write your article, using words from task L above, and the outline below. (160-180 words)

Article Outline

Paragraph 1	Introduce the main subject. Make the reader want to read more.
Paragraphs 2 and 3	Develop your article, using topic sentences and giving reasons and examples.
Paragraph 4	Finish off the article, giving the reader something to think about.

Unit 18 People

A Look at the photographs. Describe them and the relationships they show.

What is your relationship like with your brothers and sisters or your parents and grandparents?

Reading Link

B Read quickly through the two letters. What relationship is the writer having problems with, and what advice is given in the reply?

Ask Aunt Andrea

How Desperate R U?

Dear Aunt Andrea

I'm writing to you because I don't know who to ask for advice. I read your column every week, and I think that you give very good advice. It's obvious that you really understand the problems that teenagers have.

My problem is quite simple, but it's ruining my life. I don't get on with my parents. They are driving me mad! I have tried to please them, but they never seem to be satisfied with what I do. Sometimes it gets so bad at home that I feel like walking out on them. I'm getting on well at school, so that isn't the problem.

I really don't know what is to blame, but I always seem to be arguing with them. I can't do anything right. I wish they would leave me alone. Whenever I go out they're really nosy, they want to know who I am going to be with, where I am going, and when I am going to be home. It isn't fair! I don't ask them where they're going when they go out!

Last night, I stormed off because they were interfering in my private life. I've been going out with my boyfriend for three months, and everything was fine, apart from my parents, that is!

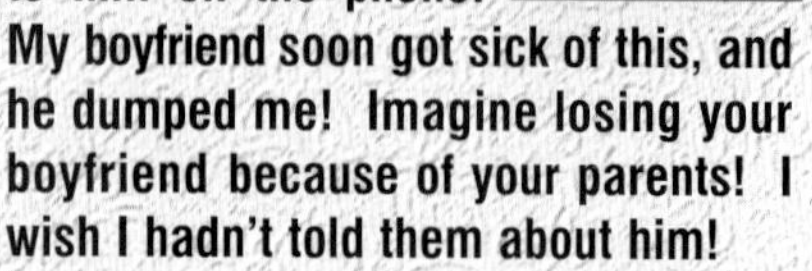

When we're on speaking terms, everything is fine, but when we argue, they won't even let me talk to him on the phone! My boyfriend soon got sick of this, and he dumped me! Imagine losing your boyfriend because of your parents! I wish I hadn't told them about him!

Sometimes I wish I was an orphan! I do love my parents, don't get me wrong, but I don't know what I should do to make the situation at home bearable. I can't go on like this. Please help me. I don't know what to do!

Yours
Desperate

Dear Desperate

Thank you very much for your letter. I am really sorry to hear that things are bad at home. However, if you take my advice seriously, the situation will get a lot better.

Under the circumstances, I think we should look at your relationship with your parents. In your letter, you don't mention whether the problem is mainly with your mum, or your dad, or both. If you get on better with one parent, try talking to him/her first. You say in your letter that you can't please them, but have you asked them what they expect from you?

You must remember that, above all, your parents love you. When they ask you where you are going, and who you are going out with, they are doing this because they care about you. I know it's tough; you feel like an adult, but to them you're still their little girl! So, don't feel that they're not giving you your freedom – they're just showing that they love you!

As for the phone calls, why don't you try to come to an agreement with your parents? You could try to explain that it makes your life really difficult if you can't answer the phone, and perhaps you could agree on a time when you can use the phone. As for your boyfriend, I hate to say this, but he can't be very understanding if he stopped seeing you just because you can't speak to him on the phone.

To sum up, I think you all agree that things can't continue in the same way. Try to talk to your parents more. If you know what they want, and they know what you want, you should all get on a lot better.

Best wishes
Aunt Andrea

C Choose the best answer for these questions about the letters.

1 Why does Desperate want to leave home?
- a She is making her parents mad.
- b She can't please her parents.
- c She has got problems at school.
- d She is ruining her parents' lives.

2 When she goes out, her parents don't ask
- a where she is going.
- b when she will return.
- c who she will be with.
- d what she is going to do.

3 Why did Desperate lose her boyfriend?
- a Her parents never let her use the phone at the weekend.
- b Her parents sometimes stop her from using the phone.
- c Her parents told her that she couldn't see him anymore.
- d She had been going out with him for three months.

4 Aunt Andrea thinks
- a Desperate's parents see her as a young girl.
- b Desperate is an adult with her own mind.
- c Desperate's parents are interfering.
- d Desperate's parents don't love her.

5 What should Desperate do about the phone? She should
- a make her parents let her use it all the time.
- b not use it at all when there is an argument.
- c arrange a time when she can use it.
- d come to an agreement with her boyfriend.

6 What does Aunt Andrea think about Desperate's boyfriend? She thinks
- a he understands how Desperate feels.
- b he can't speak on the phone.
- c he isn't a caring person.
- d he was right to stop seeing her.

Vocabulary Link

D Use these words from the letters to complete these sentences.

bearable, expect, circumstances, interfere, satisfied, storm off, situation, tough

1 Don't speak to Sam like that; you know he'll .... again!

2 I know it's .... when you're the new boy at school. Don't worry though, I'm sure you'll make lots of new friends soon.

3 I never .... in your business, so leave me alone!

4 Under the ...., it's not surprising that they fell out!

5 It's almost .... at home now that my big sister has moved out!

6 I don't know what you .... the new teacher to be like; I bet she's a real dragon!

7 My parents are .... with my school work, thank goodness!

8 The .... at home is awful; my mum and dad argue all the time.

E Can you match the expressions from the letters with their meanings?

1 drive somebody mad
2 be on speaking terms
3 get sick of
4 dump somebody
5 be nosy

a become bored with
b want to know what others are doing
c be talking to somebody
d make somebody very angry
e stop having a relationship with somebody

F Now match the phrasal verbs with their meanings.

1 get on with somebody
2 walk out on somebody
3 get on
4 fall out with somebody
5 care about somebody/something

a be concerned or worried
b leave somebody suddenly
c quarrel or argue
d have a friendly relationship with
e make progress

G Use some of the expressions and phrasal verbs from Tasks E and F to complete these sentences. Make sure you put them in the correct form!

1 My neighbours and I are not close friends, yet, but we ....

2 I asked my mother to stop .... – she keeps reading my diary.

3 Most of my friends .... well with their parents.

4 Mary .... her best friend in the summer and they haven't spoken since.

5 Helen and Tracy .... well at school since they got a new class teacher.

6 Why .... what your friends think of you? Their opinion is important.

Grammar Link

Wishes

Read this example from Desperate's letter.

*Sometimes I **wish** I **was** an orphan!*

Is this a wish about something in the present or the past? ....
What tense is the verb which follows **wish**? ....
....

Now read this sentence.

*I **wish** I **hadn't told** them about him!*

Is this a wish about something in the present or the past?..
What tense is the verb which follows **wish**? ....
Did Desperate tell her parents about her boyfriend?
....

In one part of the letter, Desperate complains. Read this sentence.

*I **wish** they **would leave** me alone.*

What is the form of the verb which follows **wish**?
....

Now complete the following rule.

Wish is followed by a past tense when we talk about something in the .... and by a .... tense when we talk about something in the past. When we use **wish** to talk about things we don't like other people doing, **wish** is followed by .... and the infinitive without **to**.

Study the Grammar Reference on page 111 before you do the task.

H Use the verbs in brackets to complete the following sentences. Make sure the verb is in the correct form: affirmative or negative.

1 She wishes she .... (choose) the red dress yesterday. Her mother says it makes her look ridiculous.

2 I wish I .... (think) of that. It's a great idea to invite your brother to stay.

3 I wish you .... (drink) your tea so noisily. It's so annoying.

4 I wish I .... (have) some money. I would really like to go to university.

5 I wish you .... (keep) your room clean and tidy. It's always in a terrible mess!

6 He wishes he .... (live) so near a busy road. Visitors always have a problem finding a parking space when they go to see him.

Listening Link

I You will hear a conversation between a radio interviewer and a student counsellor talking about young people and their relationships. For questions 1-5, complete the notes which summarise what the speakers say. For questions 6-8, fill in the correct facts.

1 Strong family relationships stop teenagers ....

2 Young people from broken homes are more at risk of ....

3 The biggest problem facing young girls is ....

4 Boys are not as likely to .... as girls.

5 Most teenagers just need ....

6 .... of teenage marriages end in divorce within a year.

7 People who get married after the age of .... are more likely to stay together.

8 Only .... in .... of the student population gets help from a counsellor.

Speaking Link 

J Look at these photographs of people in different relationships. Compare and contrast the photos, saying why you think they are behaving in this way.

A

B

I think the first/second photograph shows … .
They look as if/though they … .
Perhaps they … .
He/She might have … .
They probably wish they had … .

Writing Link 

K Imagine that you are one of the people in photograph B.

The last time you saw your friend who is studying in London, you had a terrible argument and you want to apologise. As your friend doesn't have a phone, you decide to write a letter, saying that you are sorry.

Read the letter below and fill the blanks with a preposition.

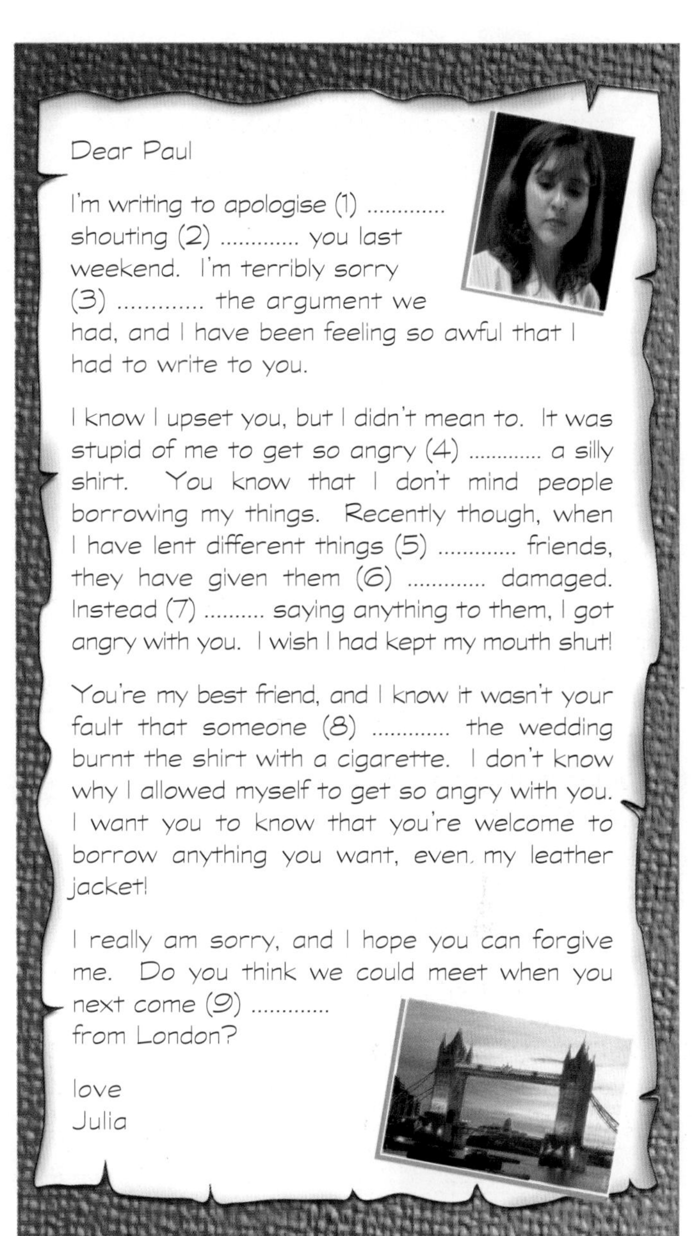

Dear Paul

I'm writing to apologise (1) .... shouting (2) .... you last weekend. I'm terribly sorry (3) .... the argument we had, and I have been feeling so awful that I had to write to you.

I know I upset you, but I didn't mean to. It was stupid of me to get so angry (4) .... a silly shirt. You know that I don't mind people borrowing my things. Recently though, when I have lent different things (5) .... friends, they have given them (6) .... damaged. Instead (7) .... saying anything to them, I got angry with you. I wish I had kept my mouth shut!

You're my best friend, and I know it wasn't your fault that someone (8) .... the wedding burnt the shirt with a cigarette. I don't know why I allowed myself to get so angry with you. I want you to know that you're welcome to borrow anything you want, even my leather jacket!

I really am sorry, and I hope you can forgive me. Do you think we could meet when you next come (9) .... from London?

love
Julia

L Now write your own letter, using the outline and the expressions below. (160- 180 words)

Letter Outline

Greeting	Dear (Paul)
Paragraph 1	Say why you are writing.
Paragraph 2	Apologise about the argument and explain why you said what you said.
Paragraph 3	Try to make up for what you said.
Closing paragraph	Apologise again and suggest that you do something together soon.
Signing off	Love (Julia)

Helpful Expressions

I'm writing to apologise for …
I'm really / terribly sorry about …
I know that I upset you, but I didn't mean to.
I really am sorry, and I hope you will forgive me.

B

C

H

A Unscramble the letters to find words related to newspapers and television and then match the words to the pictures.

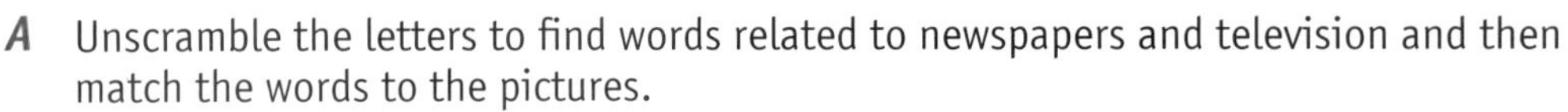

1 aerweth fecarots ( ) ( )

2 hadeeilns ( ) ( )

3 aops peora ( ) ( )

4 zqui whos ( ) ( )

5 juronailst ( ) ( )

6 corsswdro ( ) ( )

Reading Link

B Now read the article quickly and find out why listeners are surprised when they listen to one of the shows produced by *Radio Billabong.*

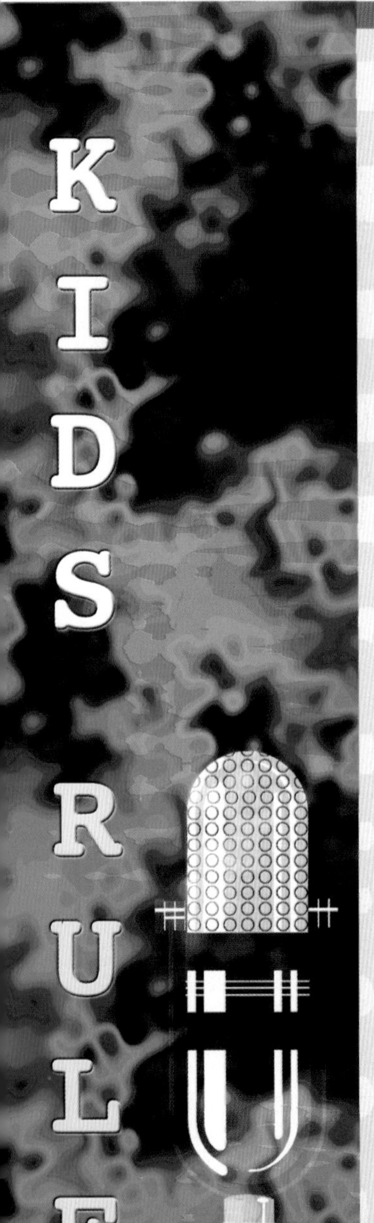

Australia has a history of using community radio stations to help children living far away from city areas to do their school work. **1** ______ *For the last eight years, it has been training children as young as seven to run the station themselves.*

Radio Billabong thinks that the community's young children should learn to take responsibility for the content and presentation of their programmes. **2** ______

On a quick visit to Billabong's studios one evening, I found about 50 kids from the age of 7 to 17 busy working on different parts of their regular evening show called Kids Rule the Airwaves. **3** ______ *The sound engineer was an experienced 10-year-old, Mike Philips, who informed me that he had been 'working' at Billabong for two years.*

When listeners tune into the daily show, they are pleasantly surprised by the quality of the programme – not only technically, but also in terms of the variety and range covered. **4** ______ *Children even younger than her have learnt to be storytellers (mostly sharing original work they have written themselves) and comedians for the 'Laugh A Minute' spot. The show goes out live, so there can't be any mistakes!*

5 ______ *Like a nervous mother just before the Christmas pantomime, Steve admits that there is really nothing to worry about. When he first started working with the children, he thought they, too, should have been nervous. But, over the years, it has been seen that children respond very positively to their new roles and gain a huge amount of self confidence. They carry out their tasks very professionally and even keep the few adults around on their toes. While I was interviewing Steve, he suddenly said: 'I'd better get down to Studio 3 as we're about to go on air.' He had been given the signal to go by 9-year-old programme manager, Des Stone.*

After further investigation, I discovered that Billabong takes on about 20 young people a year and offers them training in their chosen area. **6** ______ *Of course, they shouldn't have worried about upsetting local teachers – the teachers themselves admit that since the children have started working on Radio Billabong their academic performance has improved.*

Teachers and parents recommend their children for the training programmes and selection procedures are very strict. Steve Wright says, 'We encourage equal opportunities and also try to get a balance of ages. Younger children are proud to have the support of their family and friends and the older ones know that the skills they learn will be a definite advantage when they start their search for work later on. We believe kids ought to have the opportunity to focus on what they're interested in doing.'

Radio Billabong's aim is to open up other stations around the world. **7** ______ *So, who knows, maybe you'll be volunteering soon to help produce your own show.*

C The sentences below were removed from the article you have just read. Choose which sentences fill the gaps 1-7. There is one extra sentence which you do not need to use.

- **A** Proof of this is in the excellent training courses it offers for all jobs connected with producing a programme.
- **B** Researcher Kelly Wan is only sixteen, but she has learnt how to collect information and put it together for the news presenters.
- **C** This will allow young people in different countries to network on commercial radio and TV stations.
- **D** Children are carefully selected and the radio station has always made sure that nobody misses their regular education.
- **E** But Radio Billabong has gone one step further.
- **F** Billabong's manager, Steve Wright, at the age of 35, is responsible for organising the training and supervising the final production of the show.
- **G** The presenter of the show was 15-year-old Sean Hagen, and 11-year-old Tina Rice was responsible for taking care of the listeners' phone calls.
- **H** His mother also works on the show.

Vocabulary Link

D These words and phrases are in the article. Circle the closest meaning for each one.

1 rule (para 3)	a control b measure
2 keep sb on his/her toes (para 5)	a don't let anybody sit down b make somebody ready for anything
3 go on air (para 5)	a start presenting a programme b go somewhere by aeroplane
4 take on (para 6)	a give somebody a job b be responsible
5 procedures (para 7)	a methods b the correct way
6 proof (sentence A)	a a list of reasons or excuses b facts that show something is true

E Complete the sentences below with the correct form of the word in capitals.

1. The next show takes us one step .... towards finding our national crossword champion. ***FAR***
2. They will find out for .... how good the radio programme is. ***SELF***
3. Amanda's .... was excellent – and she's only 8 years old. ***PRESENT***
4. 'Can you call the sound ....? These mikes are not working.' ***ENGINE***
5. Bob was .... surprised when he saw how well his daughter read the news. ***PLEASANT***
6. The TV magazine gave us a lot of useful .... about the programmes on the new channel. ***INFORM***
7. The weather forecasters seem to be getting .... every year. ***YOUNG***
8. I think the best .... are my two children – they seem to have a joke for every occasion. ***COMEDY***
9. Alison was very .... before the show went on air – I could see her hands shaking. ***NERVE***
10. You need a lot of self .... in order to present a live radio show. ***CONFIDE***

Grammar Link

Modals – Advice

Read these examples from the article.

... the community's young children ***should*** *learn to take responsibility for ...*

... kids ***ought to*** *have the opportunity to focus on what they are interested in doing.*

What form of the verb do we use after **should** and **ought to**? ....

Do **should** and **ought to** have the same meaning? ....

Now read this sentence.

*'****I'd better*** *get down to Studio 3 as we're about to go on air.'*

What is **'d** short for? ....

What is the form of the verb after **'d better**? ....

Remember

Should, ought to and **had better** are used here to give advice.

Now read these examples.

... they, too, ***should have been*** *nervous.*

... they ***shouldn't have worried*** *about upsetting local teachers ...*

In the first example, were the children nervous? ....

In the second example, did they worry? ....

Complete the following rule.

We use **should** or **should not** with .... and the .... participle to talk about the past. When we say **I should have done something**, it means that it was the right thing to do but I .... do it. When we say **I shouldn't have done something**, it means that it was not a good idea to do something, but I .... it.

Study the Grammar Reference on page 111 before you do the task.

F Complete the following sentences with **should/ought to** or **had better** and the verbs in brackets in the correct form. Some of the sentences will use the negative form!

1. Trevor .... (watch) so much television – he goes to bed late and is tired at school.
2. You .... (talk) to the press. They don't always write exactly what you say.
3. You .... (listen) to the radio quiz show every week as it will help you increase your general knowledge.
4. You .... (leave) earlier. Now you are not going to arrive at the studio on time.
5. The programme manager .... (tell) us what time we are going to be on air.
6. We .... (ring) the radio station to see if they had any more information about the plane crash.
7. Peter .... (write) that article in the newspaper. Everybody is complaining about it.
8. I .... (take) the job at the TV studios – I don't like getting up so early every morning.

Speaking Link

G Work with a friend. Look at these passages. Where would you expect to see them? Give reasons for your choices.

specialist magazine article

live radio broadcast

live TV broadcast

The first passage is definitely part of a ... .
This can't be from a ... because ... .
This one must be part of a ... because ... .
I think it's from a ... because ... .

1

And you'll understand by the noise that the superstar has just arrived in her long black limousine. It's very difficult to describe the crowd's reaction; people are pushing forward to get a closer look.

2

Most professionals would agree that it's not worth trying to make adjustments to your stereo unless you really know what you are doing. So you had better note the addresses and phone numbers on page 132.

3

Fighting went on all night again last night in the centre of Beirut. Our foreign correspondent for the Middle East was there, and with great risk to her personal safety, has managed to send us the following report. 'As you can see, ...'

Listening Link 

H Listen to five people talking about their jobs and then match the speakers to the jobs (**a-f**) below. There is one extra letter that you will not use.

a TV cameraman	Speaker 1 ☐
b manager of a radio station	Speaker 2 ☐
c newspaper editor	Speaker 3 ☐
d actor	Speaker 4 ☐
e journalist	
f sound engineer	Speaker 5 ☐

Writing Link 

In Unit 16, you learnt about writing reports that give suggestions or make recommendations. In this unit, you are going to learn about writing a report that discusses a general subject. This means that you have to think of lots of ideas on the subject, and then decide what you should put in each paragraph.

HINTS

What most students like about reports is the fact that you do not need to use lots of linking words, but this does not mean that you don't need to think about what to write and how to write it. In Unit 16, you learnt that using headings makes a report clear and easy to read. This is also true of this kind of report.

I Look at the question and the report below and complete the outline using the sentences given.

Imagine that you have just received a letter from your penfriend. Read part of her letter carefully, and then write the report for her school project.

You see, we're doing a project on the media and we've decided to ask students from other countries to write reports for us about teenagers and the media in their country.

It's quite easy, really. All you have to do is write about what teenagers in your country watch on TV, which kinds of newspapers and magazines they read and what they listen to on the radio. You should also say what the most and least popular forms of media are with teenagers in your country.

To: Peter Anderson
From: Rebecca Smart
Date: 30 October 2001
Subject: Media Project

Teenagers and the Media in my Country

Introduction

The purpose of this report is to inform other teenagers about the media and teenagers in my country.

Television

1 There is very little time for teenagers to watch TV on weekdays, but at weekends, most young people watch music programmes and American series, such as *Friends*.

2 Most teenagers watch the independent channels, not those which are run by the state.

Newspapers and Magazines

1 Very few teenagers read newspapers regularly. However, there are some young people who read sports papers.

2 Young people spend a lot of money on magazines. The most popular ones are music magazines and computer magazines.

Radio

1 Most teenagers listen to the radio frequently and for hours on end. Some of them even listen to the radio while they are doing their homework!

2 The most popular radio stations are the ones which play non-stop music.

Conclusion

On the whole, radio is the most popular form of media, while newspapers are the least popular.

Report Outline

Introduction ☐

Main paragraphs ☐ **and** ☐

Conclusion ☐

a Use headings for each paragraph, and number the different points within each paragraph.

b Summarise your ideas, saying what you think are the most and least popular forms of media.

c Say what you are going to write about.

d Discuss each form of media in a separate paragraph.

J Now write your own report, using your own ideas. (160-180 words)

1	special	cartoon	a
2	well-written	effects	b
3	animated	cast	c
4	star-studded	script	d
5	simple	plot	e

A Match the adjectives with the nouns to form phrases connected with the cinema.

Reading Link

B Read the film reviews through quickly and say which actor gives the best performance, according to the critic.

TEEN MOVIE CHOICE

A *The Girl Next Door*

Stars Steve Hanson, Jackie Lamb, Peter Munroe
Director Geoff Steiner

Steve Hanson stars as a shy young man who adores his wonderful next door neighbour (Lamb), but just can't find a way to tell her how he feels. Then, fate gives him a helping hand. His wise old grandfather (Munroe) dies, leaving him millions of dollars in his will, but only if he gets married before his younger cousin. He sees this as an opportunity to get closer to Lamb, but he is afraid she will turn him down. When his old girlfriends hear about his grandfather's will, they all beg to marry him. Of course, Hanson knows that true love is only next door, and he is afraid that it might be too late, especially when his cousin meets Lamb at a party.

The plot is not new, but Lamb and Hanson make every word and emotion feel real. It's as if they're in a different, better movie.

B *The Mysterious White Lady*

Stars James Turner, Geraldine Walters, Kathy Moore
Director Pablo Garcia

Tom Ripley (James Turner) is sent to Mexico by his wealthy wife, Helen (Kathy Moore), to bring back their son, Tabor, whose life she believes is in danger. When Tom finds Tabor, he discovers that he is in trouble with the police. They think he has stolen some valuable paintings and that he is ready to do anything to hide his crime. It is only when a mysterious woman (Geraldine Walters) gets in touch with Tom that he realises that Tabor has been mistaken for somebody else.

Most of the film takes place in Mexico and it is brilliant; you won't be able to forget it easily.

C *The Rain Forest*

Stars Leslie Conway, Violet Lemonstre, Richard Carlisle
Director Dennis Bowers

Brazil's Forestry Commission was given £100,000 to allow this film to be made there. The film company even had tons of rubbish removed from two small villages, and this also cost them a lot of money. Martin (Conway), a young Australian traveller who is fed up with his life, goes in search of new experiences. He decides to stay in a small village rather than in the noisy city. When Martin has his hair cut, he learns from the barber that there is a secret paradise hidden in the jungle. He finds the place and, sadly, finds it is not all he hoped it would be.

The production and script are fantastic. Conway's acting is superb and he is well supported by a mostly unknown cast.

D *Rocket Alibi*

Stars Mark O'Toole, Tara Finnie, James Foster
Director Ted Bellamy

When the boss of a rocket manufacturing company dies, his son Darren (O'Toole) takes over. Darren's best friend, Alistair (Foster), is the company's Scottish accountant who discovers that they owe a huge sum of money to a foreign government and that they need some cash fast. Alistair then goes off to Russia to do business with some people he believes are members of the Russian Mafia. Meanwhile, Darren concentrates on his personal life back home.

The film is difficult to follow because there is just too much left unexplained. Sadly, it is a reminder of the bad old days of British films.

C Find the answers to the following questions by reading through the film reviews. Write the letters A-E in the boxes.

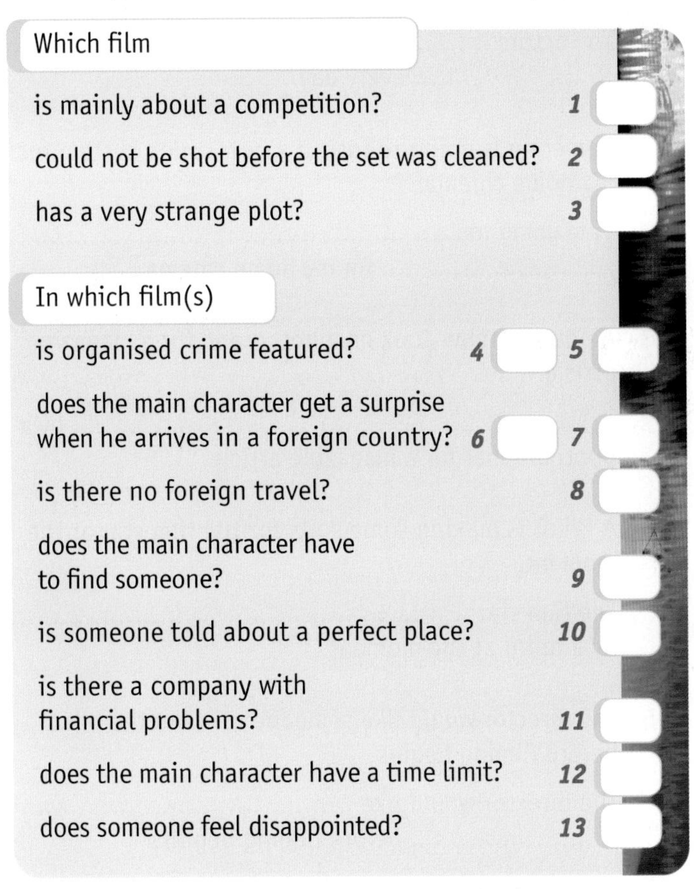

Which film

is mainly about a competition? 1 ☐

could not be shot before the set was cleaned? 2 ☐

has a very strange plot? 3 ☐

In which film(s)

is organised crime featured? 4 ☐ 5 ☐

does the main character get a surprise when he arrives in a foreign country? 6 ☐ 7 ☐

is there no foreign travel? 8 ☐

does the main character have to find someone? 9 ☐

is someone told about a perfect place? 10 ☐

is there a company with financial problems? 11 ☐

does the main character have a time limit? 12 ☐

does someone feel disappointed? 13 ☐

E *The Little Chef*

Stars Carl Fox, David Evans, Frances Fisher, Mary McGovan
Director Keith Alwyn

Charles Mackay (Fox) is a chef from Edinburgh who is known as the best in Scotland. So, he is not surprised when he is invited to the World Gourmet Cook Competition in California. When he arrives in America, he finds himself mixed up in a Mafia plot to kidnap the winner. As he is determined to win the prize for himself, he gets a member of the audience to help him deceive the kidnappers.

The film has its good moments, but the plot is unbelievable. However, the characters are full of life, so perhaps the film is worth watching just because it is so different.

Rating System

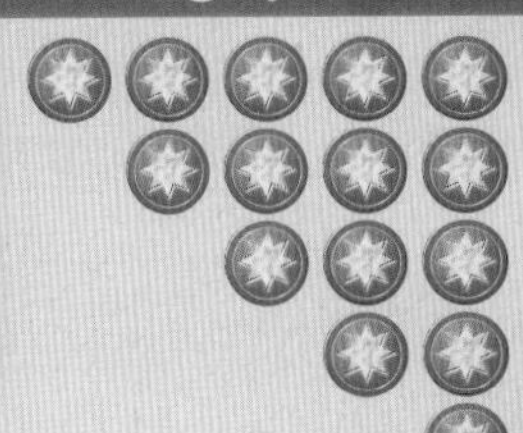

Stars	Rating
5	Don't Miss!
4	Very Good
3	Worth Watching
2	Not Very Good
1	What a Load of …!

Vocabulary Link

D The words and phrases below have been taken from the film reviews. Circle the word or phrase closest in meaning to each one.

1 adores (review A)	a loves and respects very much b likes
2 will (review A)	a order b legal paper
3 turn somebody down (review A)	a reject somebody b attack somebody
4 gets in touch with (review B)	a holds b makes contact with
5 fed up with (review C)	a bored with b excited by
6 Meanwhile (review D)	a At the same time b After a while
7 characters (review E)	a letters b people

E Circle the word that completes the sentences correctly.

1 In his latest adventures, Doctor Z has to find a **way / place** to tell George that he needs an operation.

2 All the video equipment was **robbed / stolen** when thieves broke into the studio.

3 The actors were **more / mostly** young models who wanted to star in a cheap film.

4 The director left because they **own / owe** him a lot of money.

5 Jerry won a **prize / price** for his film script for teenagers.

6 The company **borrows / lends** them an expensive car for each new film.

7 Nobody would **let / allow** them to make a film near the new lion cubs.

8 You'll have to ask somebody **other / else** to take the leading role in your new film as Jack is busy.

Grammar Link

The Causative Form

Read these two examples from the reviews.

*When Martin **has** his hair **cut** ...*
*The film company even **had** tons of rubbish **removed** ...*

Does the phrase ***has** his hair **cut*** mean that Martin does it himself, or that someone else cuts it for him?

....

....

What is the difference between these two sentences?

a *Martin **has** his hair **cut** once a month.*
b *Martin **cuts** his hair once a month.*

....

....

Complete the following reminder.

The causative talks about actions done by someone else. We use the verb .... followed by an object and a past participle.

Study the Grammar Reference on page 111 before you do the task.

F Change these sentences into ones with a causative form, without changing the meaning.

1 A hairdresser styles the actors' hair every day.
The actors ....
.... every day.

2 Someone is going to install a new sound system for my home cinema.
I am going to ....
.... for my home cinema.

3 A photographer took my photograph for a magazine article.
I .... by a photographer for a magazine article.

4 A tailor is making some suits for the film star at the moment.
The film star ....
by a tailor at the moment.

5 The director would like someone to clean the beach before filming begins.
The director would like ....
.... before filming begins.

6 A technician checked my video system last Friday.
I .... by a technician last Friday.

7 Someone has cleaned the star's dressing room very well.
The star .... very well.

Listening Link

G Listen to Kate Warner answering questions about her acting career. For questions 1-6, tick (✓) the boxes to show whether the sentences are **true** or **false**.

	T	F
1 Kate's mother encouraged her to start acting.		
2 She started acting on television before moving into cinema.		
3 She won an Oscar for her part in *Blue Mountain.*		
4 Kate doesn't like comedy roles.		
5 Other actors enjoy working with Kate.		
6 She would like to have a special part in a film written for her.		

Speaking Link

H Work with a partner. Discuss these questions.

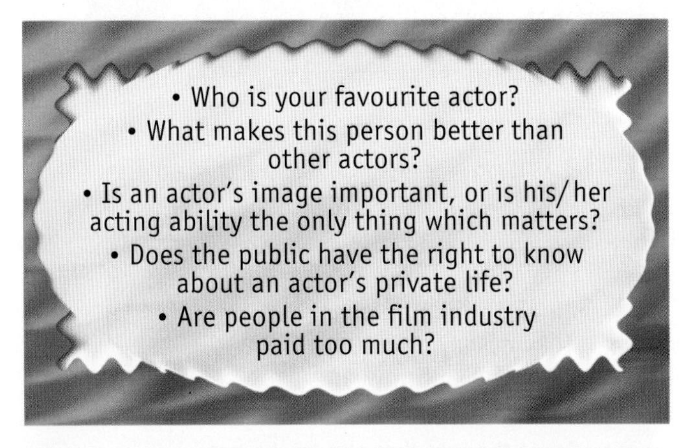

HINTS

If you can't think of anything to say, think about what other people would say. For example, what would a director or a cinema-goer say?

Now report back to the class.

Writing Link

I *Imagine that a local newspaper has announced that it will be sponsoring a film festival at a cinema in your area. Look carefully at the announcement from the newspaper and the outline below and put the letter opposite in the correct order.*

The Daily Rag and XYZ Cinema are proud to announce the first annual

Maintown Film Festival.

We would like to know what you, the readers, want to see at the festival.

THE READER WITH THE BEST SUGGESTIONS WILL WIN TICKETS TO TEN FILMS OF THEIR CHOICE.

32018

Letter Outline

Greeting	Dear Sir
Paragraph 1	Thank the newspaper for asking for the readers' opinions. Give your reason for writing.
Paragraphs 2 and 3	Group your ideas together in organised paragraphs, and say why you think your suggestions will be popular with other readers.
Closing paragraph	Thank the newspaper again. Say that you hope that the film festival will be a great success.
Signing off	Yours faithfully (your name)

A ☐

I would like to thank you again for asking for your readers' opinions. I hope that the film festival will be a great success.

B ☐

Yours faithfully
Martin Jones

C ☐

Dear Sir

D ☐

Firstly, I believe that the films to be shown at the festival should be popular films with well known actors. People in our town don't like watching films that nobody has heard of, but you could show old favourites as well as new films.

E 

I was very happy to read about the Film Festival. I would like to thank you for giving us the opportunity to give our opinions. I have some suggestions to make which, I hope, other readers will agree with.

F 

I also think that it would be a good idea to have talks by famous actors and directors, as people could learn more about the film industry. Finally, holding competitions and parties is always a good way to interest the public.

J Now write your letter using the outline and the example to help you. (160-180 words)

Review 5 Units 17 18 19 20

Complete the following story by putting one word in each space.

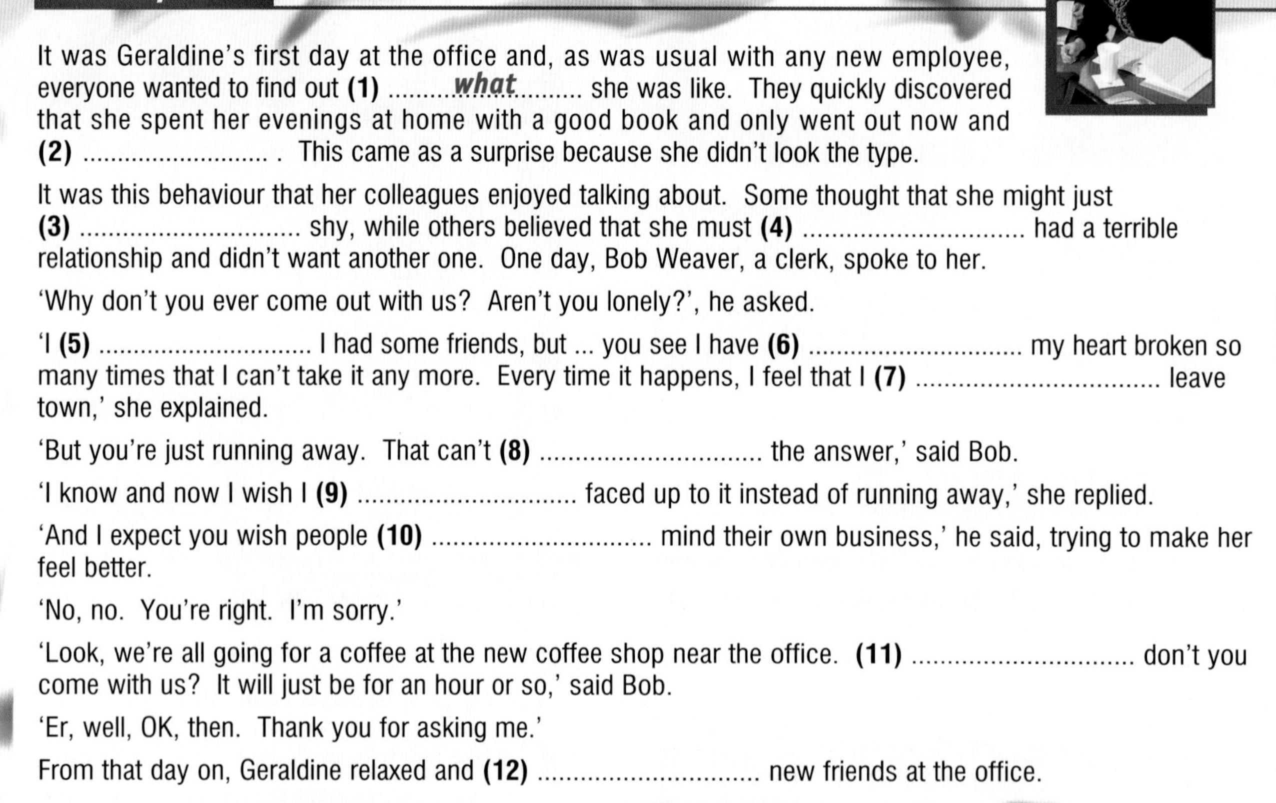

Lonely Girl

It was Geraldine's first day at the office and, as was usual with any new employee, everyone wanted to find out **(1)** ....*what*......... she was like. They quickly discovered that she spent her evenings at home with a good book and only went out now and **(2)** .... This came as a surprise because she didn't look the type.

It was this behaviour that her colleagues enjoyed talking about. Some thought that she might just **(3)** .... shy, while others believed that she must **(4)** .... had a terrible relationship and didn't want another one. One day, Bob Weaver, a clerk, spoke to her.

'Why don't you ever come out with us? Aren't you lonely?', he asked.

'I **(5)** .... I had some friends, but ... you see I have **(6)** .... my heart broken so many times that I can't take it any more. Every time it happens, I feel that I **(7)** .... leave town,' she explained.

'But you're just running away. That can't **(8)** .... the answer,' said Bob.

'I know and now I wish I **(9)** .... faced up to it instead of running away,' she replied.

'And I expect you wish people **(10)** .... mind their own business,' he said, trying to make her feel better.

'No, no. You're right. I'm sorry.'

'Look, we're all going for a coffee at the new coffee shop near the office. **(11)** .... don't you come with us? It will just be for an hour or so,' said Bob.

'Er, well, OK, then. Thank you for asking me.'

From that day on, Geraldine relaxed and **(12)** .... new friends at the office.

Use the words given in capitals at the end of each line to form a word that fits in the space.

Bill and Penny Black

Bill and Penny **(1)** ....*believe*....... they have been writing to each other for about four years.	***BELIEF***
They had met in what you might call rather **(2)** .... circumstances. Bill helped	***USUAL***
to clean the local theatre. Although there was no **(3)** .... between them, they	***RELATION***
both had the same surname: Black. Nobody ever took Penny **(4)** .... when she	***SERIOUS***
told everyone her name was Penny Black. She had gone to see a **(5)** .... of	***PERFORM***
King Lear because her teacher at school had asked her to do a **(6)** .... on one	***PRESENT***
of Shakespeare's plays. Going to see the play was a **(7)** .... opportunity for her	***VALUE***
to meet the leading actor. When she went to meet him, she saw the **(8)**	***ACCOUNT***
stealing money from the safe. She went and **(9)** .... Bill, who called the police. When	***FIND***
Penny moved to **(10)** .... town soon after, she and Bill continued to write to each other.	***OTHER***

Rewrite the second sentence so that it has a similar meaning to the first one. Use the word in bold to rewrite the sentence.

1 Someone is going to fit new locks on my door.
have
I am going ....to have new locks fitted.... on my door.

2 There's no doubt that the police gave the journalists some details of the crime.
must
The police .... the journalists some details of the crime.

3 It's a shame I don't have the talent to be an actor.
wish
I .... the talent to be an actor.

4 It would be a good idea for you to apologise to Mark immediately.
better
You .... to Mark immediately.

5 Perhaps they aren't getting on with each other at the moment.
might
They .... on with each other at the moment.

6 Someone took my photo for the magazine article yesterday.
had
I .... for the magazine article yesterday.

7 It really annoys me when Maggie makes nasty comments.
stop
I wish Maggie .... nasty comments.

8 Sandra thinks it's a pity she didn't buy a better TV.
wishes
Sandra .... a better TV.

In each sentence below, there is one extra word. Circle the word that is not needed.

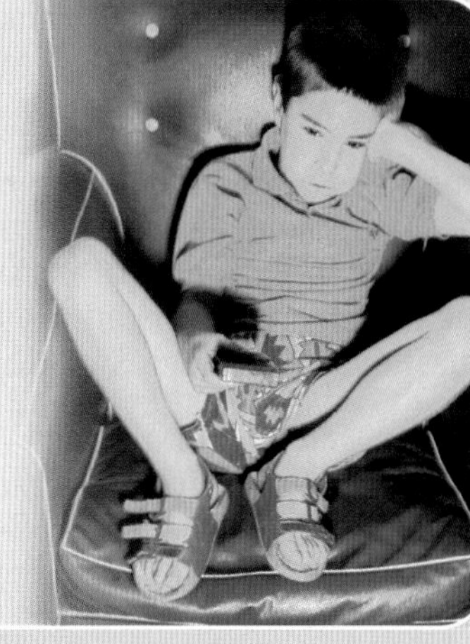

1 He can't have to made another film – he died three years ago.
2 The burglar must have been broken into the house over the weekend.
3 I wish I had had seen how they made the video.
4 The newspaper editor should have finished up with the article by now.
5 Terry was having a new lock fitted in after the burglary.
6 Barbara and Harry wish they had got married in the spring when the weather it was warmer.
7 Should I buy a TV guide when I will go to the newsagent's?
8 Don't you wish you had reminded hers your aunt that it was your birthday?
9 I finally had the TV be fixed, so you can now watch your favourite programmes.
10 They shouldn't have leave the ladder outside when they go on holiday.

Circle the words that complete the sentences correctly.

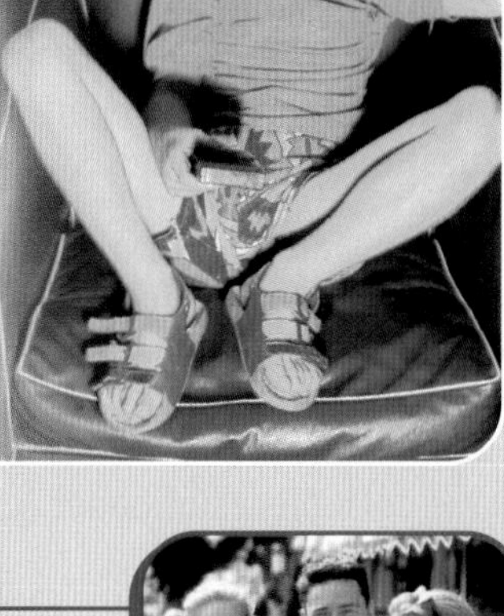

1 The police stopped him for drinking and driving and he lost his driving **diploma / licence**.
2 If you ask Mary she will give you some **advise / advice** about your problem.
3 Are you **expecting / waiting** your relatives to come for Easter?
4 My grandmother always told me to take every **opportunity / occasion** when it came my way.
5 There is a **live / life** interview on TV tonight with the famous actor from *Beverley Soap*.
6 Aaron had to leave work early so that he didn't **miss / lose** the beginning of the film.
7 I always give my neighbour a helping **arm / hand** when she isn't feeling well. She lives alone.
8 The editor sent out a **remember / reminder** to all the journalists to say that her office hours were from 9 am to 1 pm.

Project Work

The Estate Agent's

Draw a plan of your home, then on another piece of paper, write about it, describing it in such a way that the people who read the description will want to buy it. Give your first piece of work to your teacher, who will return it to you with advice and suggestions. Make any changes and when you are finally happy with it, display all the plans and descriptions around the classroom. Look at the display and decide which home you like best. Work with a friend and tell him/her which house you have chosen and why.

Job Centre

You are going to create a job centre in your classroom. A job centre is a place where people who don't have jobs are able to look for work or ask for advice about training. They can also get help with writing their CV (a paper which gives details of a person's qualifications, work experience, interests, etc) or learning how to be successful at interviews.

This activity should be done in pairs. Your teacher will give you a job advertisement to look at together. You will need to think of what kind of person would apply for the job which is being advertised and also what kind of questions an employer would ask at an interview.

In your pairs, write a short CV for a suitable employee and also a list of questions that an employer might ask someone at an interview. When you have finished, give your work to your teacher, who will comment and make some suggestions. When you have made any changes, give both pieces of paper to another pair.

You will be given two pieces of paper from another pair. In pairs, decide which of you will play the role of employer (the person interviewing) and future employee (the person applying for the job). Then look at the interview questions or the CV and think about what you will say.

When you are ready, the dialogues can be acted out in front of the class, who will decide if the future employee gets the job.

Music Survey

Bring in an English song of your choice, and let the rest of the class hear it. Before the lesson, make arrangements with your teacher to get copies of the lyrics for all the students and your teacher. Be prepared to say a few things about the song: who it is sung/written by, when it was released, etc. Remember, you should also be able to tell the class why you like the words or music of the song you have chosen.

Fashion Show

Working in pairs, make a note of what your partner is wearing. You should write a commentary of the clothes and accessories he/she is wearing, describing them fully. Ask your teacher for any vocabulary you may need. Your teacher will give you an example of the style of language that you can use.

Tourist Guidebook

As a class, decide what you would like to see in a tourist guidebook for your city/town/village. There are some suggestions below. Work with a partner or in groups. Each pair/group should gather information on one or two topics. Decide how many pages will be needed for each topic. Remember to give your first pieces of work to your teacher before adding any pictures/postcards etc; there's no point doing lots of hard work only to find that changes are necessary, and that you must cut or tear them out.

Suggested topics for a tourist guidebook

Where to stay	Nightlife
Where to eat	Places of historical interest
Shopping	Places of general interest
Entertainment	Don't miss ... !

When your teacher has seen your work, and has given advice or suggestions, you can finally prepare your page(s) for the tourist guidebook. When all the pages have been prepared, put them together in a logical order. You could also make a contents page, and number the pages, so that it is easier for other people to read. Display your tourist guidebook in the class/school.

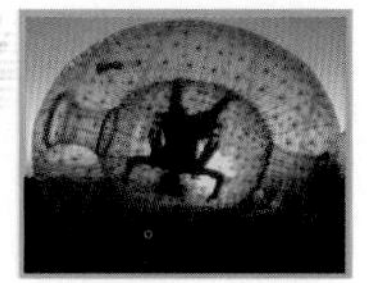

The Rules of the Game

Work with a partner or in groups. Collect information about a sport or hobby you are all interested in, and make a poster to be displayed in the class/school. You must explain what the hobby/sport involves and what equipment is necessary. Try to find out some unusual information about your sport/hobby.

Remember to give your first pieces of work to your teacher before adding any pictures. Your teacher will tell you when you should present your poster to the rest of the class. Remember, you should be able to say a few words about it: why you are interested in this sport/hobby, how long you have been playing/supporting it, etc.

Weather Survey

Work in teams of four. Collect information from the newspapers (either in English or your own language) about the weather for a period of one week. Compare the weather in your country with the weather in three other countries in different parts of the world. Make bar charts, pie charts or graphs to show the differences in, for example, the amount of sunshine, temperature, rainfall, etc. Your teacher will show you some examples. Write a paragraph explaining what you have found. The results (the charts and the writing) from each team can be displayed on the classroom wall.

Clean-up Outing

Why not organise an activity to clean up your neighbourhood? Your class could get people to help you clean up a local park or children's playground. You could arrange it for a Saturday or Sunday morning and get some of your friends to come along.

In class, you can form a committee to

- decide what you are going to do, and when (date and time).
- design a poster to let people know.
- make a list of organisations who might want to help you.
- write a notice for the local English newspaper.
- decide who will do what on the day.
- make a list of equipment needed.

On the day, you will need to wear rubber gloves so you don't get your hands dirty. You and your teacher will divide everyone into groups and give each team a large plastic rubbish bag. Each group should go to a different area of the park/playground and see how much rubbish they can put in their plastic bag. There might even be a prize for the winning team who collects the most! Your teacher will be able to help you with other ideas.

Unit 9 Health and Fitness

Fitness Programme

Work in pairs. One student plays the role of a person who needs some advice about changing their lifestyle/diet or following a fitness programme while the other student plays the part of a fitness adviser. Your teacher will tell you which situation card to look at.

You should read the situation card with your partner and work out a dialogue. This can be practised and then acted out in front of the rest of the class. You should include information about food, exercise and any habits that need changing.

Situation Card 1

Susan is a 25-year-old nurse who works in a local hospital. She has just moved to the town and doesn't know many people. She works shifts, which means sometimes she works during the day and sometimes at night. She doesn't earn a lot of money.

Situation Card 2

David is a 45-year-old factory manager. He smokes a packet of cigarettes every day and is a bit overweight. His doctor has told him to change his habits as he is at risk of heart disease.

Situation Card 3

Mark is an elderly man who has had a heart attack. He's recovered well and has been told by his doctor that he should be careful about what he eats and do some light exercise.

Situation Card 4

Jenny is a university student. She is living away from home and has found cooking for herself difficult. She usually eats junk food because it is quick and easy. She has noticed that she is putting on weight.

Situation Card 5

James is 36 years old and works in an office. He spends most of his time sitting down. He works long hours and has a wife and two young children.

Situation Card 6

Helen is 29 and she has just had her first baby. She feels tired and fat and doesn't have much time to cook for herself or her husband. Her mother lives about 5 minutes away from her house.

Unit 10 Public Services

Lending Library

Date Borrowed	Name	Class	Book	Author	To Be Returned	Date Returned
24-10-01	*J Smith*	*A Class*	*BFG*	*Roald Dahl*	*14-11-01*	*10-11-01*

Set up a library in your class/school. You can use your own books or school books, if available. Make sure that the books are clearly labelled with the owner's name. First of all, you must make a list of all the books in your library. It helps if they are grouped according to their level, so pupils can find the books which they can understand. Different coloured stickers can be used to show the different levels.

Then the books should be displayed somewhere appropriate. A shelf or a bookshelf/cupboard would be best. Remember that it should be positioned in such a way that it is easy for everyone to get to, but it shouldn't disturb anyone. Use a different section/shelf for each level.

Use the notebook to make a note of who borrows the books from the library and when they borrow them. You should also agree on a borrowing time; that is, how long the pupils should be able to keep the books. It's a good idea to divide the pages into columns, as shown in the example above.

Rather than letting everyone write in the book, some of the pupils in your class can be librarians. It will be their job to show pupils the books which are suitable for them, and to write down the details in the notebook. They will also be responsible for putting any returned books back in the right place, and checking that pupils don't keep books for too long.

Then you should decide when your lending library will open. This will depend on how many librarians there are and when they have time to work in the library. When you have decided, make a poster to advertise your lending library and put it up on the school noticeboard. Happy reading!

Unit 11 Transport

Survey

In this activity, you will need to work in pairs or small groups. Each group prepares a questionnaire about different means of transport. Your group should think of multiple choice questions such as:

1. Which form of transport do you most often use?
   a bus **b** train **c** trolley **d** taxi **e** private car
2. If you were travelling to an island for your holidays, would you choose to travel
   a by ferry? **b** by plane? **c** by hydrofoil?

When your group has prepared its questionnaire, you can interview the rest of the class. The results of your survey can be transferred to a graph and displayed in the classroom. Your group should write a short paragraph or two to explain your results.

Unit 12 Travel

Holiday Brochure

You should bring photographs/pictures of hotels, beaches and holiday destinations to class. Choose one that you would like to write about. You should include information about location, accommodation, things to do and see and prices. Give your work to your teacher who will make comments and suggestions about it. Then make a small poster, including the photograph/picture and the necessary information. These can be displayed in class or around the school.

The Door-to-door Salesperson

Role-play in pairs. One of you will be a salesperson who goes from one house to another trying to sell a useful product. The other will be somebody who answers the door. The salesperson's job is to persuade the person at home to buy the product. You can work in pairs to invent a product.

Think about

- what it is (think of adjectives you will use to describe it).
- what it does.
- how it works (you might want to show the person).
- cost.
- reasons why somebody should buy your product.

The person in the house should think of ways to reply to the salesperson. Even if you decide to buy the product, you will still have to arrange how you are going to pay, etc.

When you are ready, each salesperson should move to another customer and try to sell his/her product.

Cookery Competition

Write a recipe for a simple dish or a drink (something which does not need cooking). Use the outline below. Give your first piece of work to your teacher, who will return it to you with advice and suggestions. When all the students are happy with their final pieces of work (you may like to illustrate yours), your teacher will arrange a suitable time for the cookery competition. You should bring all the necessary ingredients and equipment with you.

When all the students have prepared their recipes, try the food/drink and give it a mark from one to ten. When the competition is over, and the winner has been announced, display the recipes in the classroom/school.

Recipe 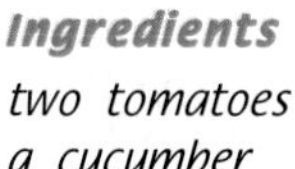 *Outline*

You will need

a chopping board
a knife
a big bowl
etc

(List the equipment, one item under the other.)

Ingredients

two tomatoes
a cucumber
a red pepper
etc

(List the food needed to make the dish, again, one item under the other.)

Method

1 Wash all the vegetables.
2 Slice the red pepper.

(Using numbered points, explain how to make the dish. Remember to use the imperative.)

The Ideal School

You will need to work in groups. You are going to create an ideal school. First of all, you need to discuss what the school will be like (which subjects will be taught, which facilities you want).

When you have a list of points that you want to include, decide who will work on the timetable of lessons and who will work on the extra activities/facilities available.

You should remember that students at the school need to be able to survive in the real world when they have finished their education, so a timetable full of music, sport and dance lessons might not be the best!

When you have come up with a timetable and facilities available, your group could design a poster or leaflet advertising your school and what it offers. These could be displayed in the classroom.

SPRING TERM YEAR 1					
DAY/TIME	Mon	Tue	Wed	Thu	Fri
9^{00} - 9^{45}					
9^{45} - 10^{30}					
10^{30} - 10^{45}		B R	E	A	K
10^{45} - 11^{30}					
11^{30} - 12^{15}	*Basketball*	*Tennis*	*Gym*		
12^{15} - 1^{15}		L U	N	C	H
1^{15} - 2^{00}					
2^{00} - 2^{45}					

Small Ads

Invent a gadget or device which you think other people would find useful.

Make an advertisement for your gadget.

- Draw a diagram of your gadget,
- label its features, and
- write a short paragraph describing it in such a way that the people who read the advertisement will want to buy it.

Remember to give your first pieces of work to your teacher to see before you present your advertisement to the rest of the class.

The Trial

Your teacher will give you instructions when you have finished reading the information below.

What happened: An old lady was caught shoplifting a few days before Christmas. She had taken some small toys and put them in her bag without paying.

People

The Accused (old lady)

Christmas is coming and you don't have very much money to buy presents for your grandchildren. You feel terribly sorry about what happened. When the manager of the shop stopped you and asked to look in your bag, you didn't let him and now he thinks you were trying to hide the toys you had in your bag. After he discovered them, he called the police. You say that, although you had put the toys in your bag, you were going to pay for them before leaving the shop.

Witness (shop manager/owner)

You are fed up with people stealing things from your shop and feel very pleased that one of them has been caught. You hope the court will make an example of the old lady so other people will be discouraged from stealing.

Witness (shop assistant)

You work in the toy shop full time. You saw the old lady put several things into her bag. You feel sorry for her but decided to tell your manager, who called the police.

Police Officer

You were called to the toy shop by the manager, who was very pleased that one of his shop assistants had caught a thief. You interviewed the old lady and decided to arrest her.

Defence Lawyer

It is your job to provide evidence that the old lady is not guilty.

Prosecution Lawyer

It is your job to prove the old lady is guilty.

Judge

It is your job to manage the trial. You must call witnesses and summarise the case to the jury before they decide on their verdict.

Jury

You must listen to all the evidence and make up your minds as to whether the old lady is guilty or not.

Counselling

Work in pairs. In this activity, one student plays the role of a person with a problem and the other student plays the role of the counsellor. Your teacher will tell you which situation card to read. Now act out the situation. The student with the problem should explain the problem to the counsellor, and the counsellor must give the best advice he/she can.

Situation Card 1

Mike is really worried that he is going to fail his exams, which are in two weeks. He hasn't done any revision at all. He knows that his parents expect him to do really well, which makes him feel even worse.

Situation Card 2

Tracy has got the lead role in the end-of-year school play. She is really excited about it. (She wants to go to drama school when she finishes high school.) But she also wants to go on the school trip to France, which is during the last week of term. All her friends are going, and she thinks it will be great fun.

Situation Card 3

Tim really wants to get a part-time job so that he can save up to buy a motorbike. His best friend's father owns a fast food restaurant, and he has offered him a job. However, his mother thinks his school work will suffer and she won't let him ride a motorbike because she says it's too dangerous.

Situation Card 4

Joanna had an argument with her best friend a month ago, and she has been very unhappy since then. She knows that she was to blame, and she wants to make up with her friend, but she doesn't know how to start.

Situation Card 5

David has just moved to a new town and a new school. He really misses his friends, and feels really lost at school. His parents say that he will soon make new friends, but he doesn't think so.

Situation Card 6

Tina has been invited to a party but she is very shy. She knows that a boy called Jack will be there and he always makes fun of her. Tina's friends keep telling her she must go to the party, and she doesn't know what to do.

Situation Card 7

Sam is 17 years old and has very strict parents who won't let her go out without her brother. She really wants to go to a party at the weekend, but she doesn't want to go with her brother, because her friends make fun of her.

Unit 19 The Media

Class Newspaper

Make a class newspaper using the project work you have done throughout the year. Some of your work can go in the paper as it is (*The Estate Agent's*, Unit 1, *Small Ads*, Unit 16, etc), while other work may need to be written. For example, someone could write an article about the *Cookery Competition* (Unit 14). You may also add anything else you would normally find in a newspaper (weather reports, horoscopes, etc).

When your teacher has seen your work, and given advice or suggestions, you can make your final edit; this means, prepare your page(s) for the newspaper. When all the pages have been prepared, put them together in a logical order. Display your newspaper in the class/school. (Your teacher might like to get your newspaper photocopied to show other classes at school.)

The Awards

This should be done in two lessons.

First lesson: The nominees

As a class, suggest three films for each category. Each student should make at least one suggestion. (Remember, if your choice wins, you must make a short speech accepting your 'award', and saying something about the film.) You must then vote for which film you think is the best in each category. Use the form your teacher gives you. Your teacher will collect the forms and tell you in the next lesson which film in each category has won. At home, you must prepare your speech(es) for the film(s) you have chosen.

Second lesson: And the winner is ...

Your teacher will announce the winners of each category. If you win, go to the front of the class to 'accept' your award and give the speech you have prepared.

Grammar Reference

Unit 1

1.1 Present Simple

We use this tense for • things which are true in general. • the laws of science and nature. • how often something happens.	*Many people **live** in the heart of the city.* *In winter, some trees **lose** all their leaves.* *Linda **cleans** her house twice a week.*
This tense is used with the **stative verbs** opposite which appear only in simple forms.	*believe, belong, hate, hear, know, like, mean, need, prefer, remember, seem, suppose, understand*
Do and *does* are used to form question and negative forms of this tense.	***Does** she **share** a bedroom with her sister?* *I **don't like** living near this busy road. It's very noisy.*

1.2 Present Continuous

We use this tense for • actions that are in progress at the time of speaking. • actions that are in progress around the time of speaking.	*Michael **is painting** the kitchen at the moment.* *They **are saving up** to buy a new carpet.*

Remember: **We don't use this tense with stative verbs (see 1.1).**

1.3 Adverbs of Frequency

Adverbs of frequency are used to say how often something happens. They come before the main verb, but after the verb *be*.	*We **always** leave the light on at night.* *I am **never** late for school.*
Here are some common adverbs of frequency.	*always, never, often, rarely, seldom, sometimes, usually*

1.4 Question Tags

Question tags are short questions at the end of a positive or negative sentence. We use question tags • when we want someone to agree with what we are saying. • to make sure that what we are saying is right. They are formed with modal and auxiliary verbs.	*She walks to work, **doesn't she?*** *They lived in Glasgow, **didn't they?*** *He won't make the curtains, **will he?*** *You can send a fax, **can't you?***
Note how these question tags are formed.	*Let's go, **shall we?*** *I'm a good player, **aren't I?*** *Stay here, **will you?***

Remember: **When *have* is used as a main verb, we use the verb *do* to make the question tag.**
You have a two-bedroomed house, don't you?

Unit 2

2.1 Past Simple

We use this tense for • a state or completed action in the past when the time is important. • a series of completed actions in the past.	 *She **passed** her driving test last month.* *We **sold** the house two years ago.* *He **sat** down, **took out** a pen and **started** writing.*
Did is used to form question and negative forms of this tense.	***Did** you **send** them a postcard when you were on holiday?* *They **didn't watch** TV last night.*

Spelling Rules

1 Most regular verbs in the Past Simple are formed by adding *-ed*. Verbs ending in *-e* add *-d*.	*look* *save*	*looked* *saved*
2a Regular verbs ending in **consonant-vowel-consonant** double the consonant before the ending *-ed* when the stress is on the final syllable.	*stop* *prefer*	*stopped* *preferred*
2b When the stress is **not** on the last syllable, the final consonant is not doubled.	*visit*	*visited*
3 Regular verbs ending in *-l* double the *-l*.	*travel*	*travelled*
4a Verbs ending in a consonant and *-y* change the *-y* to an *-i* before the ending *-ed*.	*carry*	*carried*
4b When the verb ends in a vowel and *-y*, the *-y* doesn't change.	*play*	*played*
Note that these verbs do not follow the spelling rules. For a list of irregular verbs, see page 112.	*lay* *pay* *say*	*laid* *paid* *said*

2.2 Past Continuous

We use this tense • for actions that were in progress at a certain time in the past. • for two or more actions that were in progress at the same time in the past. • for an action that was in progress in the past and was interrupted by another action. • to describe things in the past.	 *We **were playing** cards at 10 o'clock last night.* *Amy **was writing** a letter when I arrived.* *I **was washing** the floor and Jack **was working** in the garden.* *I **was writing** a letter when my boss arrived.* *The reporters **were asking** the film star questions.*
This tense often follows *as* and *while*.	*The lights went out **while** she **was typing**.*

Remember: **We don't use this tense with stative verbs (see 1.1).**

Unit 3

3.1 Future Simple

We use this tense to • make predictions, promises and threats. It is often used with the verbs like *think* and *believe*, as well as phrases like *I am sure ...* .	 *I think an astronaut **will walk** on Mars in the next twenty-five years.* *I am sure you **will like** the new CD.*
• offer to do something for someone.	*I **will give** you a lift to the concert.*
• ask someone to do something.	***Will** you **turn** the music down, please?*
• make a sudden decision.	*'What can I get for Jane? I know. **I'll get** her a CD.'*

3.2 Present Continuous with a future meaning

We use this tense for plans and arrangements that have been made for the future.	*We're **having** a ballet lesson after work.*

Remember: We don't use this tense with stative verbs (see 1.1).

3.3 *be going to*

We use *be going to*	
• for plans and arrangements for the future.	*They **are going to see** that new rock band tonight.*
• to make a prediction for the near future based on a present situation.	*Mark's band has got the highest score. They **are going to win** the talent contest.*

3.4 Future clauses with *when*

• Future tenses cannot be used in a future clause with *when*. We use a present tense.	*I'll give her your message **when** she **wakes up**.* *I'll go to the bank **when I've got** the money.* *I'll listen to my new CD **when I'm driving** to work.*
• The same is true of future clauses with *as soon as, after, before, until, while* and *by the time.*	*She'll give you a ring **as soon as** the musician **arrives**.*

Unit 4

4.1 Modals – Ability, Obligation and Necessity

• We use *can* to talk about ability in the present. It is followed by a verb without *to*. The negative form of *can* is *cannot or can't.*	*She **can** design hats quite well now.* *She **can't** change my bag because I've lost the receipt.*
• We use *could* to talk about ability in the past. It is followed by a verb without *to*. The negative form of *could* is *could not (couldn't).*	*He **could** run quite fast when he was at college.* *We **couldn't** find a bag to match the dress.*
• We use *be able to* to talk about ability in other tenses.	*She **hasn't been able to** model since March.* ***Will** you **be able to** get a job if you go to the UK?*
• We use *must* to talk about obligation and necessity. It is followed by a verb without *to*. The negative form of *must* is *must not (mustn't). Mustn't* means you're not allowed to do something.	*We **must** take photos of Jane during the fashion show.* *You **mustn't** steal other people's designs!*
• The past form of *must* is *had to.*	*I **had to** stay late at work to finish making the dress.*
• We also use *have to* to talk about obligation and necessity. The negative form of *have to* is *don't have to*. *Don't have* to means you can choose whether you do something or not.	*I **have to** buy a new dress for the wedding.* *You **don't have to** wear a skirt; you can wear trousers.*
• The past form of *have to* is *had to.*	*We **had to** repair the necklace.*

4.2 *Although, despite, in spite of*

• We use *although, despite* and *in spite of* to talk about something which is unexpected because of certain facts.	***Although she is** tall, she wears high heels.* ***Despite/Inspite of having** the best models, the fashion show was a disaster.*
• We use *although* with a subject and a verb.	***Although it was** very cold, he didn't wear a coat.*
• We use *despite* and *in spite of* with a noun or a verb in the gerund form (*-ing*).	***Despite/Inspite of having** a lot of money, she rarely buys expensive clothes.*

5.1 Present Perfect Simple

We use this tense for	
• completed actions and states when the time is not important. There is a connection with now.	*I've **stayed** at that hotel before so I know what it's like.* *She**'s worked** in Sydney so she knows what to expect.*
• actions and states that started in the past and are still true now.	*I **have lived** here since 1989.* *We **have worked** in this city for over ten years.*
This tense is used with *already, just* and *yet*.	*They have **already** been to the Sahara.* *He's **just** heard the news. Have you heard about it **yet**?*

Remember: **See page 112 for a list of irregular verbs.**

5.2 Present Perfect Continuous

We use this tense	
• for actions which began in the past and have recently stopped.	*He's tired because he**'s been working** in the garden.*
• to say how long something has been in progress.	*She **has been studying** geography for two years.*

Remember: **We don't use this tense with stative verbs (see 1.1).**

5.3 *have been to, have gone to*

• We use *have been to* when somebody has visited a place and has come back.	*Michael **has been to** London many times, so he can recommend somewhere to stay.*
• We use *have gone to* when somebody is visiting a place and hasn't come back yet.	*Susan **has gone to** France, but she'll be here next week.*

5.4 *for* and *since*

• We use *for* and *since* with the Present Perfect tense to talk about how long an action has been in progress or how long a state has existed until now.	*They've been taking their holidays in Cornwall **since** they were children.* *I've been in Russia **for** two weeks and I'll stay until the end of the month.*
• *Since* is followed by a specific point in time.	*We have stayed in this hotel every summer **since** 1995.*
• *For* is followed by a period of time.	*Kate hasn't had a holiday **for** three years.*

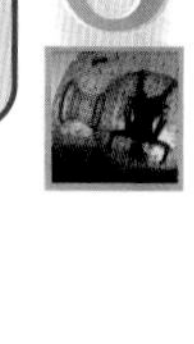

6.1 Past Perfect Simple

We use this tense for an action or state which existed before another event, state or time in the past.	*I **hadn't played** baseball until I went on holiday to America.* *By the time we arrived, the match **had** already **finished.***

Remember: **See page 112 for a list of irregular verbs.**

6.2 Past Perfect Continuous

We use this tense for actions which were in progress until a certain time in the past.	*We **had been sitting** in the stadium for about an hour when the team came onto the pitch.*

Remember: **We don't use this tense with stative verbs (see 1.1).**

7.1 Passive

We use the passive when we are more interested in the action than who or what is responsible for it (the agent). The table below shows how some active verb forms change to passive verb forms.

Tense	Active Form	Passive Form
Present Simple	*take/takes*	*am/are/is taken*
Present Continuous	*am/are/is taking*	*am/are/is being taken*
Past Simple	*took*	*was/were taken*
Past Continuous	*was/were taking*	*was/were being taken*
Present Perfect Simple	*have/has taken*	*have/has been taken*
Past Perfect Simple	*had taken*	*had been taken*
Future Simple	*will take*	*will be taken*
Modals	*must take*	*must be taken*
Infinitive	*to take*	*to be taken*
Gerund	*taking*	*being taken*

The passive is formed with the verb *be* and a past participle.

We change an active sentence into a passive sentence in the following way. The object of the verb in the active sentence becomes the subject of the verb in the passive sentence. The verb *be* is used in the correct form together with the past participle of the verb main in the active sentence.

They have never recorded rain in this area.
Rain ***has never been recorded*** *in this area.*

In this example we do not know who has recorded the rain and the information is not very important so we do not include the word *they* in the passive sentence.

Sometimes we want to know who or what is responsible for the action. In a passive sentence the word *by* comes before this information.

The sun heats the earth during the day.
The earth ***is heated by*** *the sun during the day.*

7.2 Adjectives ending in *-ing* or *-ed*

- Adjectives which describe things, places, situations, events and people end in *-ing*.
- Adjectives which describe how someone feels end in *-ed*.

The thunderstorm was ***amazing****.*
Listening to the weather forecast is ***boring****.*

I was ***interested*** *in the experiment.*
She was ***surprised*** *to see snow in June.*

8.1 Adjectives: Word Order

When we use two or more adjectives, we usually put them in a set order.

opinion, size, age, shape, colour, nationality, material + noun

Look at those ***lovely pink*** *flowers she planted.*
I don't like that ***big square plastic*** *box you bought.*

8.2 Comparatives and Superlatives

We use the comparative and superlative form of words to compare two or more places, people or things. We make comparatives and superlatives in the following ways:

• We usually add *-er/-est* to adjectives/adverbs with one or two syllables.	tall fast	taller faster	tallest fastest
• The last consonant is doubled for one syllable adjectives with **consonant-vowel-consonant.**	hot red	hotter redder	hottest reddest
• For one or two syllable adjectives/adverbs that end in *-y*, the *-y* changes to *-i* before we add *-er/-est.*	dry happy early	drier happier earlier	driest happiest earliest
• We use *more/most* or *less/least* with adjectives/adverbs of more than two syllables.	sensible carefully	more/less sensible more/less carefully	most/least sensible most/least carefully

Some adjectives/adverbs are irregular and the comparative and superlative forms shown in the table below must be learnt.

Adjective/Adverb	Comparative	Superlative
a lot of	more	most
bad(ly)/ill	worse	worst
far	farther/further	farthest/furthest
few	fewer	fewest
good/well	better	best
little	less/smaller	least/smallest
many	more	most
much	more	most
old	older/elder	oldest/eldest

• We use *than* with the comparative when two people, groups, places or things are compared.	*Tigers are **more** dangerous **than** rhinos.*
• We can also make comparisons using *(not) as* + adjective + *as.*	*The Indian elephant is **not as big as** the African elephant.*

9.1 Reported Speech (statements)

When the reporting verb is in a past tense, the tenses used by the speaker usually change as follows:

Direct Speech	Reported Speech
Present Simple *'I **want** an ice cream,' she said.*	Past Simple *She said (that) she **wanted** an ice cream.*
Present Continuous *'He **is working out** in the gym,' she said.*	Past Continuous *She said he **was working out** in the gym.*
Present Perfect Simple *'We **have** never **played** tennis,' they said.*	Past Perfect Simple *They said they **had** never **played** tennis.*
Present Perfect Continuous *'I **have been dieting** for two weeks,' he said.*	Past Perfect Continuous *He said he **had been dieting** for two weeks.*
Past Simple *'I **put** your trainers in the cupboard,' said John.*	Past Perfect Simple *John said he **had put** my trainers in the cupboard.*
Past Continuous *'She **was preparing** a salad for lunch,' he said.*	Past Perfect Continuous *He said she **had been preparing** a salad for lunch.*

We also make other changes.

can *'I **can't** go with you because I am too tired,' said Mark.*	*could* *Mark said he **couldn't** go with me because he was too tired.*
may *'I **may** go to the health club later,' he said.*	*might* *He said he **might** go to the health club later.*
must *'I **must** get more sleep,' she said.*	*had to* *She said she **had to** get more sleep.*
will *'He **will** be tired after training,' she said.*	*would* *She said he **would** be tired after training.*
don't *'**Don't** touch the gym equipment because Pete will get angry,' said Wendy.*	*not to* *Wendy told me **not to** touch the gym equipment because Pete would get angry.*

Note that when we talk about something which is still true or is a fact, the tenses do not change.	*'London **is** the capital of England,' our teacher told us.* *Our teacher told us that London **is** the capital of England.*

Sometimes there are changes in time and place in reported speech. Changes are as follows:

Direct Speech	Reported Speech
today *'I'll start my exercises* ***today****,' he said.*	*that day* *He said he'd start his exercises* ***that day****.*
yesterday *'I arrived early* ***yesterday****,' she said.*	*the day before* *She said she had arrived early* ***the day before****.*
last week/month/year/etc *'He saw his doctor* ***last week****,' she said.*	*the week/month/year/etc before* *She said he had seen his doctor the week before.*
tomorrow *'I'll buy the vitamins* ***tomorrow****,' she said.*	*the following day* *She said she'd buy the vitamins* ***the following day.***
next week/month/year/etc *'The gym will open* ***next month****,' he said.*	*the following week/month/year/etc* *He said the gym would open* ***the following month****.*
ago *'He joined the gym two years* ***ago****,' she said.*	*before* *She said he had joined the gym two years* ***before****.*
now *'He's learning golf* ***now****,' he said.*	*then* *He said he was learning golf* ***then****.*
at the moment *'We're eating salad* ***at the moment****,' they said.*	*at that moment* *They said they were eating salad* ***at that moment****.*
this/these *'****These*** *are my football boots,' he said.*	*that/those* *He said* ***those*** *were his football boots.*
here *'He's been waiting* ***here*** *for an hour,' she said.*	*there* *She said he'd been waiting* ***there*** *for an hour.*

Remember: **We do not use speech marks with reported speech.**

9.2 Other reporting verbs

Sometimes we use other verbs to report speech.

agree/refuse/decide/offer + verb with *to*	*'I will come with you to the dentist,' she said.* *She* ***agreed to come*** *with me to the dentist.*
apologise + *for* + verb in the gerund form (*-ing*)	*'I'm sorry I arrived late,' she said.* *She* ***apologised for arriving*** *late.*
blame + object + *for* + verb in the gerund form (*-ing*)	*'Brenda caused the accident,' said Alice.* *Alice* ***blamed*** *Brenda* ***for causing*** *the accident.*
accuse + object + *of* + verb in the gerund form (*-ing*)	*'Larry stole the tennis racket,' said Alec.* *Alec* ***accused*** *Larry* ***of stealing*** *the tennis racket.*
suggest + *that* + subject + (*should*) + verb without *to*	*'Why don't you go to the beach, Paul?' said Carol.* *Carol* ***suggested that*** *Paul* ***should go*** *to the beach.*
suggest + *that* + subject + verb in the Past Simple	*'You should see a doctor, Mark,' said Jane.* *Jane* ***suggested that*** *Mark* ***saw*** *a doctor.*
Note that *suggest* can be followed by a gerund when the speaker is involved in the action.	*'Let's play a game,' said Ben.* *Ben* ***suggested playing*** *a game.*

Unit 10

10 Reported Speech (questions)

The changes in tenses are the same as the ones we make in reported statements.	*See 9.1 on pages 106 and 107.*
When a direct question has a word like *who, what, how,* etc, we use this word in the reported question.	*'**Where** is the post office?' he asked.* *He asked **where** the post office was.*
When a direct question doesn't have a word like *who, what, how,* etc, we use *if/whether* in the reported question.	*'Can I send the parcel by post?' he asked.* *He asked **if/whether** he could send the parcel by post.*

Remember: **In reported questions, the verb follows the subject, as in ordinary statements. We do not use question marks.**

Unit 11

11.1 *used to, would*

We use *used to* + verb • to talk about past habits. • to talk about past states.	*She **used to go** to work by bus when she was younger.* *He **used to be** interested in old aeroplanes.*
The negative form of *used to* is *didn't use to.*	*I **didn't use to travel** by ferry, but now I go to the islands this way every summer.*
We also use *would* + verb to talk about past habits.	*He **would catch** the early morning train to work.*

Remember: **We cannot use *would* + verb to talk about past states.**

11.2 *be/get used to*

We use *be/get used to* • to talk about habits and states that are not strange or new to us. • to talk about things which became familiar in the past. They are followed by a verb in the gerund form (*-ing*) or a noun.	*Don't worry! I **am used to driving** on the left.* *She **is used to the noise** from the main road now.* *I soon **got used to flying** when I started working for an airline.*

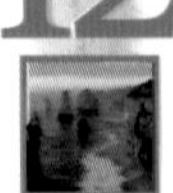

Unit 12

12.1 First Conditional

We use the first conditional to talk about things which will probably happen now or in the future. *If* + present tense, *will/can/may* + verb without *to*	***If** the weather **is** fine, we**'ll go** away for the weekend.* ***If** they **give** us the money, we **can go** to Disneyland.* *We **may go** to Corfu **if** Mary **gets** a job there.*
Unless can be used in this conditional. *Unless* means the same as *if not.*	***If** I **don't have** time to visit, I will phone instead.* ***Unless** I **have** time to visit, I will phone instead.*

12.2 Second Conditional

We use the second conditional to talk about things • that probably won't happen now or in the future. • we know will not happen. *If* + past tense, *would/could/might* + verb without *to*	***If** she **had** more money, she **would travel** first class.* *I **might** visit my uncle **if** I **had** time off work.* ***If** I **lived** nearer to the train station, I **could go** to London more often.*

12.3 Third Conditional

We use the third conditional to talk about the past. These are always hypothetical things because we cannot change the past.

If + past perfect, *would/could/might* + *have* + past participle

If *you* ***had listened*** *to the museum guide, you* ***would have learnt*** *about the paintings.*
If *we* ***had booked*** *our plane tickets earlier, we* ***could have found*** *the dates we really wanted.*
If *she* ***hadn't been*** *so ill, she* ***might have enjoyed*** *the holiday.*

Unit 13

13 Relative clauses

Relative clauses give more information about the subject or the object of a sentence. In some relative clauses the information is necessary and in others it is extra.

Relative clauses with necessary information

This type of relative clause gives us information that we need to understand who or what the speaker is talking about. We do not use commas. This type of clause is called a **defining relative clause.**

The woman ***who is paying for her bread now*** *is my godmother.*
The building ***which looks like a castle*** *is actually a shop.*
The park ***where we had our first picnic*** *is now a shopping centre.*
The man ***whose uncle is a friend of mine*** *got a job at the local supermarket.*
This shopping centre was opened in the year ***when I left school.***

Relative clauses with extra information

This type of relative clause gives us extra information. We use commas to separate it from the rest of the sentence. This type of clause is called a **non-defining relative clause**.

Mrs Brown, ***who lives next door,*** *owns a corner shop.*
Tesco, ***which is a supermarket chain,*** *has opened three new shops this year.*
She opened a shop in Paris, ***where she met her husband.***
Laura Jenkins, ***whose dress shop is very popular,*** *is thinking of retiring.*
This shopping centre was opened in 1995, ***when I was still at school.***

Unit 14

14 Future Continuous

We use this tense

- for an action which will be in progress at a specific time in the future.
- for a plan for the future.
- to find out about somebody's plans when we want to ask them a favour.

This time next week, we ***will be enjoying*** *a meal at the new Indian restaurant in town.*
*He****'ll be taking*** *a friend to dinner on Saturday.*
Will *you* ***be going*** *shopping tomorrow because I need some bread and milk?*

Remember: **We don't use this tense with stative verbs (see 1.1).**

Unit 15

15.1 Future Perfect Simple

We use this tense to talk about something that will have happened before a certain time in the future.

They ***will have finished*** *all their tests* ***by*** *the end of the week.*
He ***won't have returned*** *from the library* ***by*** *the time they arrive.*
Will *she* ***have given*** *the students their marks* ***by*** *half past one?*

15.2 Future Perfect Continuous

We use this tense to talk about how long something will have been in progress at a certain time in the future.	***By*** *this time next year, she* ***will have been studying*** *in this university* ***for*** *three years.* ***By*** *seven o'clock, I* ***will have been writing*** *reports* ***for*** *two hours!*

Remember: **We don't use this tense with stative verbs (see 1.1).**

Unit 16

16.1 Gerund

Here are some common verbs that are followed by a verb in the gerund (-*ing*) form: *admit* *keep* *avoid* *mind* *enjoy* *miss* *finish* *practise* *imagine* *risk*	*When did you* ***finish writing*** *the report?* *I don't* ***mind waiting*** *for you to finish the experiment.* *He doesn't* ***enjoy working*** *in the laboratory.* *Do you* ***miss designing*** *computer programs?* *Can you* ***imagine being*** *a famous inventor?*
Here are some expressions that are followed by a verb in the gerund (-*ing*) form: *It's not worth ...* *It's no use ...* *There's no point ...* *can't help* *can't stand*	***It's no use inviting*** *the physics teacher; she's working that day.* ***I can't stand reading*** *computer magazines.* ***There's no point buying*** *a new computer now.*
Note that we often use the gerund (-*ing*) form after prepositions.	*I am interested* ***in doing*** *a computer course.* *How* ***about going*** *to see the science museum?* *I congratulated her* ***on winning*** *the science competition.*

16.2 Infinitive

Here are some common verbs that are followed by a verb with *to* (the full infinitive): *afford* *manage* *agree* *offer* *allow* *plan* *attempt* *promise* *decide* *refuse* *fail* *seem* *hope* *threaten* *learn* *want*	*We* ***managed to find*** *a special gift for the biology teacher.* *Do you* ***want to buy*** *a chemistry set for John?* *I couldn't* ***afford to get*** *a printer for my computer.* *They* ***hope to discover*** *a new medicine this year.* *He* ***failed to find*** *a cure for the common cold.*

Note that some common verbs can be followed by either a verb in the gerund or full infinitive form without a change in meaning. For example: *begin, continue, start.*	*She* ***began cooking.*** *She* ***began to cook.***

17 Modals – Possibility and Certainty

Could and *might* are used to talk about possibility. • When we talk about the present or future, *could* and *might* are followed by a verb without *to*. • When we talk about the past, *could* and *might* are followed by *have* and a past participle.	 *He **could go** to prison for a very long time.* *She **might meet** her lawyer this afternoon.* *They **could have seen** the bank robbery on the way home last night.*
Must and *can't* are used to talk about certainty. *Must* means that we are sure something is, was or will be true. *Can't* means we are sure something isn't, wasn't or won't be true. • When we talk about the present or the future, we use *must* and *can't* with a verb without *to*. • When we talk about the past, we use *must* and *can't* with *have* and a past particple.	 *She **must be upset** because her car was stolen.* *He **can't be** guilty because he was away at the time of the robbery.* *He **must be** a policeman because he's wearing a uniform.* *It **can't have been** a man who broke into the house because the window was too small.*

18 Wishes

We use *wish* to talk about a situation or an action we are sorry about. • *Wish* is followed by a past tense when we talk about the present or the future. • *Wish* is followed by a past perfect tense when we talks about the past. • *Wish* is followed by *would* and a verb without *to* when we talk about other people's annoying habits or to say that we would like something to be different in the future. We use it for actions, not states.	*I **wish I didn't argue** all the time with my parents.* *She **wishes** she **could get** a job as a counsellor.* *I **wish** you **had come** to David's house last night.* *I **wish I hadn't forgotten** my brother's birthday.* *I **wish** you **would wash** your hands before you eat.* *I **wish** he **wouldn't speak** with his mouth full.*

Remember: **We cannot use *would* when we talk about our own behaviour.**

19 Modals – Advice

Should, *ought to* and *had better* are used to give advice. They are followed by a verb without *to*. The negative forms are *should not* (*shouldn't*), *ought not to* and *had better not*.	*He **should read** the newspaper more often.* *We **ought to watch** that new TV drama.* *They **had better get** these microphones repaired soon.* *She **shouldn't spend** so much money on women's magazines.* *You **ought not to let** them watch so much TV.* *He'**d better not miss** my first radio show tonight.*
We use *should* + *have* + past participle when we criticise our own behaviour or somebody else's. We use it to say that something was the right thing to do, but wasn't done. The negative form is *shouldn't* + *have* + past participle. We use it when we want to say that something happened although it wasn't a good idea.	*You **should have arrived** at the studio half an an hour ago. You're late!* *He **shouldn't have used** bad language on TV.*

20 The Causative Form

We use the causative form when we want to say that we have arranged for somebody to do something for us. • We use *have* + object + past participle. We can also use *get* + object + past participle.	*The film star **had** his picture **taken** for a magazine.* *She**'s going to have** her hair **cut** before the party.* *He **is getting** the costumes **made** by a famous fashion designer.*

Irregular Verbs

All the verbs in this list appear in *Link Intermediate Course Book.*

Infinitive	Past Simple	Past Participle
be	was/were	been
beat	beat	beaten
become	became	become
begin	began	begun
bet	bet	bet
bite	bit	bitten
bleed	bled	bled
blow	blew	blown
break	broke	broken
bring	brought	brought
broadcast	broadcast	broadcast
build	built	built
burn	burnt	burnt
buy	bought	bought
catch	caught	caught
choose	chose	chosen
come	came	come
cut	cut	cut
dig	dug	dug
do	did	done
drink	drank	drunk
drive	drove	driven
eat	ate	eaten
fall	fell	fallen
feel	felt	felt
find	found	found
fly	flew	flown
forecast	forecast	forecast
forget	forgot	forgotten
get	got	got
give	gave	given
go	went	gone
grow	grew	grown
have	had	had
hear	heard	heard
hide	hid	hidden
hit	hit	hit
hold	held	held
keep	kept	kept
know	knew	known
leave	left	left
lend	lent	lent
let	let	let
lie	lay	lain
lose	lost	lost

Infinitive	Past Simple	Past Participle
make	made	made
mean	meant	meant
meet	met	met
mistake	mistook	mistaken
pay	paid	paid
put	put	put
read	read	read
ride	rode	ridden
ring	rang	rung
run	ran	run
say	said	said
see	saw	seen
sell	sold	sold
send	sent	sent
set	set	set
shake	shook	shaken
shine	shone	shone
shoot	shot	shot
show	showed	shown
shut	shut	shut
sing	sang	sung
sink	sank	sunk
sit	sat	sat
sleep	slept	slept
speak	spoke	spoken
spend	spent	spent
split	split	split
spring	sprang	sprung
stand	stood	stood
steal	stole	stolen
stick	stuck	stuck
sting	stung	stung
strike	struck	struck
swim	swam	swum
take	took	taken
teach	taught	taught
tear	tore	torn
tell	told	told
think	thought	thought
throw	threw	thrown
understand	understood	understood
wake	woke	woken
wear	wore	worn
win	won	won
write	wrote	written

Word List

The number in brackets shows the unit where the word appears. If there is more than one number, it means that the word appears again with a different meaning. We use ***sb*** for *somebody* and ***sth*** for *something*.

above all (18)
abroad (2)
absolutely (13)
academic (19)
accept (2)
accessory (16)
accommodation (13)
according to (12)
account (10)
accountant (20)
accurate (7)
acid rain (8)
act (16)
actual (6)
actually (5)
adapt (16)
adaptor (13)
adjust (16)
admit (15)
adore (20)
advanced (7)
advantage (4)
adventure (17)
advertise (13)
advice (18)
advise (14)
advisory (9)
aerosol (8)
affect (7)
aim (19)
aisle (11)
alarm (16)
album (2)
alive (17)
allow (15)
alternative (17)
amazed (3)
amazing (16)
among (5)
amount (15)
animated (20)
ankle (9)
anniversary (14)
announce (11)
annoy (8)
annual (20)
antibiotics (13)
anticipate (5)
antique (13)
anything but (14)
apart from (14)
apartment (1)
apology (16)
appear (15)
appearance (4)
apply (10)
appointment (16)
appreciate (2)
approach (7, 12)
arch (5)
area (1)
argue (18)
armed (5)
army (7)
around the clock (13)
arrangement (1)
arrest (3)
arrival (12)
assistance (12)
assistant (4)
assume (13)
at hand (9)
at one's fingertips (16)
attack (17)
attitude (13)
attract (1)
audience (3)
available (2)
avoid (6)
awful (14)
backache (1)
bagpipes (3)
bakery (13)
balance (15)
balanced (4)
ban (3)
barber (20)
bargain (13)
barrel (4)
base on (13)
bearable (18)
bed linen (12)
beetroot (4)
beg (20)
beginner (7)
bench (10)
benefit (8)
bet (18)
bill (14)
bind (4)
biological clock (9)
blame (16)
blanket (14)
bleed (8)
board (9)
boarding card (11)
borrow (18)
boss (20)
bounce (6)
brainy (2)
brave (2)
break (9)
break in (4)
break the law (17)
breath (9)
breathing equipment (2)
breathtaking (5)
bride (4)
bright (13)
broadcast (19)
broken home (18)
bronze (4)
broth (14)
built into (16)
bull (14)
bunch (14)
burgle (17)
burn down (2)
business (15)
butcher's (14)
cable car (5)
calculator (13)
candle (7)
candlestick (8)
carbohydrates (9)
carriage (11)
carry out (7)
carrying cover (16)
case (13, 17)
cash (20)
cashier (13)
cast (20)
catch up (9)
catch up with (17)
catwalk (4)
cause (9, 15)
celebrate (14)
celebrity (4)
censorship (3)
century (7)
certain (5)
certificate of attendance (15)
chain (3)
change (13)
chaotic (14)
chart (7)
check in (11)
check out (5)
chemist's (13)
cheque (2)
chilled (14)
chip (16)
choice (4)
classmate (3)
clause (13)
clear (17)
clerk (12)
climate (16)
close (11)
close-up (16)
cloth (14)
coastline (12)
code (16)
coin (1)
cold (4)
collection (4)
column (18)
come to an agreement (18)
comedian (19)

Word List

comment (3)
commercial (19)
commit (17)
common (1)
common sense (7)
community (5)
compare (1)
competitive (10)
complain (1)
complaint (9)
complex (7)
comprehensive (4)
concentrate (6)
concerned about (1)
conclusion (7)
confidence (6)
confused (9)
connect (1)
connection (10)
conscience (17)
consciousness (2)
constantly (7)
contact (5, 17)
container (11)
contents (14)
contract (2)
convict (5)
convicted(17)
cool (16)
cork (14)
corkscrew (14)
corner shop (13)
correspondent (17)
cosmetics (16)
couch potato (9)
cough mixture (13)
council house (1)
counsellor (18)
count (11)
count on (14)
couple (14)
course (6)
court (3)
cramped (1)
crash (19)
crashing (12)
crater (12)
creative (2)
crew (3)
crime (5)
criminal (17)
crisp (14)
crisps (14)
critic (20)
crossword (19)
crowded (7)
cruise (11)
cub (20)
cube (14)
customer (14)
daily (16)
damage (3)
damp (1)
deadly (12)
deaf (10)
death (17)
decade (7)
deceive (20)
deck (11)
decor (4)
definitely (14)
degree (15)
delay (11)
delicatessen (14)
delighted (13)
demonstrator (15)
department store (13)
departure lounge (11)
depend (16)
depressed (7)
deserve (17)
designer (4)
designer clothes (2)
desire (5)
desperate (18)
destination (12)
destroy (8)
detailed (7)
detention (17)
development (16)
dig out (14)
dine (5)
director (20)
dirty (14)
disaster (7)
discount (16)
discourage (6)
discovery (10)
disease (9)
distance (5)
divorce (18)
DIY store (13)
do one's best (15)
do well (15)
dominate (5)
door-to-door salesperson (13)
double-check (7)
dragon (18)
drawer (16)
dressing room (20)
drip (10)
drive sb mad (18)
drop (5)
drunken (17)
due to (5)
dull (1)
dump (8, 18)
dump somebody (18)
during (4)
duty-free (11)
DVD system (16)
earn (17)
earphone (13)
editor (19)
education (15)
effect (6)
effort (14)
elderly (10)
electronic (16)
elegant (2)
emigrate (12)
emotion (20)
enable (9)
encourage (5)
encyclopaedia (16)
end up (14)
enemy (17)
engaged (3)
enormous (1)
entertainment (11)
entire (4)
equal (19)
equipment (2)
Equity Card (2)
equivalent (4)
erase (15)
estate agent (1)
even (13)
evil (17)
exchange (4)
excuse (15)
execute (17)
exhausted (9)
exhibit (4)
expect (5, 18)
expense (12)
experience (4)
experiment with (10)
expert (16)
express (15)
extremely (11)
face (15)
facilities (10)
fact (19)
factor (14)
fair (16)
fall out (18)
false economy (13)
famous (2)
fare (11)
fascinating (4)
fashion-conscious (4)
fast asleep (9)
fate (20)
fault (1)
favour (15)
favourite (11)
fear (1)
feature (16, 20)
fed up with (20)
fee (2)
feel sorry for (17)
fence (6)
festival (20)
fewer (15)
fictional (17)
field (14)
fill (12)
financial (20)
fine line (17)
fire (17)

Word List

lifestyle (9)
lifetime (4)
lightning (7)
lightweight (13)
likely (4)
limit (20)
limited to (13)
limousine (19)
literary (3)
litter (8)
live (19)
load (20)
loan (6)
local (3, 5)
location (1)
lock (1)
lock out (17)
long-range (7)
look forward to (3)
look through (6)
looks (2)
loss (9)
luxurious (1)
luxury flat (1)
lyrics (3)
mad dogs and Englishmen (14)
main (5, 13)
mainly (18)
major (13)
majority (13)
make a difference (15)
make an attempt (15)
make for (12)
make fun of (15)
make matters worse (13)
make progress (15)
make up for (17)
make up one's mind (2)
manage (4, 11)
manner (2)
manufacturer (16)
mark (9, 12)
marking (15)
match (4, 7)
material (6)
maximum (16)
meadow (12)
means of transport (11)
meanwhile (20)
measure (7, 10)
media (19)
medicine (15)
member (20)
membership card (10)
memorable (11)
mention (8)
mess (14)
mike (19)
mind (8)
minor (5)
mist (5)
mistake sb/sth for (20)
mix (8)
mix up (14, 20)
mobile phone (1)
mood (7)
motorway (13)
movie (20)
murder (17)
muscle (9)
mysterious (20)
narrow (12)
natural (7)
nature reserve (12)
neat (15)
necklace (13)
negative (2)
neither (13)
nervous (11)
neutral (13)
no longer (13)
noisy (11)
nor (13)
nothing like (13)
notice (2)
now and then (17)
nuclear reactor (8)
object (4)
obvious (15)
occasion (17)
occupant (6)
occupation (2)
official (3)
on board (11)
on display (4)
on its own (6)
on sale (6)
on speaking terms (18)
on strike (11)
on the whole (4)
on time (4)
operate (7)
operating theatre (10)
opinion (10)
opportunity (15)
order (20)
ordinary (16)
organise (16)
originally (16)
orphan (18)
Oscar (20)
other than (5)
out of breath (9)
out-of-date (16)
outdoors (14)
overhear (1)
owe (12)
owing to (17)
p & p (16)
pace (5)
pack (5)
painlessly (16)
pantomime (19)
parachuting (2)
paradise (20)
parcel (10)
part (20)
particular (5)
partly (1)
pass through (12)
passenger (17)
passport (15)
pasta (14)
pastime (2)
pâté (14)
patient (2)
pay (17)
pay a visit (4)
pay attention to (13)
pea (14)
peace (14)
peaceful (11)
pear (13)
percussion (3)
perform (11)
performance (20)
perfume (4)
permission (17)
personal (10)
pet (12)
petition (3)
picnic hamper (14)
pleasure (5)
plot (20)
pocket money (15)
point (13)
point of view (4)
point out (17)
pole (14)
polish (11)
polite (9)
polluted (8)
popular (1)
population (18)
portion (9)
possible (17)
practical (17)
predict (7)
prediction (3)
premises (3)
preparation (12)
presentation (10)
presenter (3)
press (19)
pressure (7)
prevent (4)
previous (2)
price (1)
pride (11)
prime minister (4)
printout (16)
prison (17)
prisoner (1)
private life (18)
prize (3)
procedure (19)
produce (19)
product (5)
production (20)
professional (10)
profit (15)

Word List

specialise (10)
specific (14)
spectacular (5)
spectator (6)
splash (8)
split (12)
spoil (14)
sponsor (20)
spot (7, 9, 14)
sprained (9)
spring (6)
stable (7)
staff (5)
stain (14)
star-studded (20)
state (1, 19)
steal (17)
stethoscope (10)
stick (3, 9)
stick out (9)
stick to (13)
stir-fry (14)
storm off (18)
strain (9)
strength (7)
strict (19)
strike (7)
strings(3)
struggling (2)
studio (19)
style (20)
subject (15)
suburban (10)
such as (17)
suffer (15)
sugar-starved (14)
suggest (15)
suit (4, 20)
suitable (3)
summary (15)
sunbather (14)
superb (20)
supervise (19)
supply (6)
support (2)
suppose (13)
surface (7)
surgeon (10)
surroundings (4)
survey (13)
survive (5)
suspended (17)
swarm (14)
switch off (3)
sympathise (9)
tailor (20)
take action (13)
take advantage of (13)
take care of (19)
take sb/sth for granted (14)
take off (11)
take on (19)
take over (16)
take place (13)
take shape (5)
take sth seriously (18)
take the plunge (6)
tale (1)
tambourine (3)
tangerine (13)
tanker (8)
tear (6)
technician (20)
technique (10, 16)
teenager (2)
temple (5)
tempting (13)
tense (9)
test (6)
text (10)
theft (17)
therefore (13)
thief (20)
think about sth twice (12)
threat (5)
threaten (3)
thrill (6)
thunderstorm (7)
ticket (11)
tidy (17)
tie up (4)
till (17)
tin (14)
tip (10)
tone (13)
too bad (14)
torrential (7)
toss (10)
tough (18)
town council (11)
track (3)
traditional (13)
transport (5, 6)
travel light (12)
triangle (3)
trip (7)
trust (13)
tumble dryer (6)
tune into (19)
turn (6)
turn down (2, 3)
turn one's stomach (6)
umpire (6)
under the circumstances (18)
unemployed (10)
unfair (17)
unique (11)
unlike (17)
unlimited (3)
unscramble (19)
unusual (2)
up to a point (3)
up-to-date (16)
upper (11)
upset (3, 9)
urgent (12)
useful (3)
valuable (20)
value (10)
van (17)
variety (4)
vast (4)
vegetarian (14)
vehicle (11)
veil (4)
view (12)
violence (17)
virus (16)
voice (3)
volcano (12)
volunteer (19)
vote (3)
voucher (16)
waist (4)
walk out on sb(18)
ward (10)
wardrobe (5)
warning (14)
washing machine (13)
wasp (14)
waste (4, 8)
wavy (2)
weak (13)
wealthy (1)
weapon (17)
weigh a ton (13)
weight (9)
well-built (2)
wheelchair (10)
while (11)
whole (1)
wide awake (9)
wildlife (14)
will (20)
windbreak (14)
wine (14)
wise (20)
witness (17)
wonder (6)
work experience (15)
work out (13)
workout (9)
worlds apart (1)
worth (5, 10)
wrestler (6)
yet (14)
youth club (17)

Answers to Units 9 and 10

Unit 9 Health and Fitness

Calculate your total score according to the scoring chart below and then check your score against the analysis.

Scoring

1	a 10 points	b 0 points	c 5 points
2	a 5 points	b 10 points	c 0 points
3	a 0 points	b 5 points	c 10 points
4	a 0 points	b 5 points	c 10 points
5	5 points for each choice		

Analysis

0-20 You are most definitely the biggest couch potato of them all! We're surprised you even got out of bed this morning! Hasn't anybody told you to do something healthy for a change? You must make more of an effort to get in shape, and try to think about what you eat!

25-40 OK, so you're not a couch potato, but you aren't exactly breaking any world records, are you? And have you never heard the phrase 'You are what you eat'? You would feel much better if you took more exercise and ate healthier food. (It's tastier too, you know!)

45-60 Well done! You obviously understand the importance of keeping fit. Don't overdo it though, we don't want you to collapse with exhaustion!

Unit 10 Public Services

Countries		Taxi Drivers	Waiters
1	Australia	nothing	5-10%
2	Belgium	nothing	16-20%
3	Canada	11-15%	11-15%
4	Greece	5-10%	5-10%
5	Italy	16-20%	11-15%
6	Japan	nothing	nothing
7	South Africa	5-10%	5-10%
8	Switzerland	nothing	5-10%
9	The USA	16-20%	16-20%

Credits

First published by New Editions 2001

Reprinted April 2006

New Editions
37 Bagley Wood Road
Kennington
Oxford OX1 5LY
England

New Editions
3 Theta Street
167 77 Hellinikon
Athens
Greece

Tel: (+30) 210 9883156
Fax: (+30) 210 9880223
E-mail: enquiries@new-editions.com
Web site: www.new-editions.com

Course Book ISBN 960-8136-12-1

Acknowledgements

Projects written by Gill Mackie and Sarah Bideleux.

Illustrated by Panagiotis Angeletakis

The publishers would like to thank Visual Hellas for permission to reproduce copyright photographs.

We are grateful to the following for permission to adapt and reproduce copyright material:

Zorb Limited (photographs) for Unit 6. More information can be found on their web site: www.zorb.com

Clean up Greece for parts of Unit 8. More information can be obtained on their web site: www.cleanupgreece.org.gr

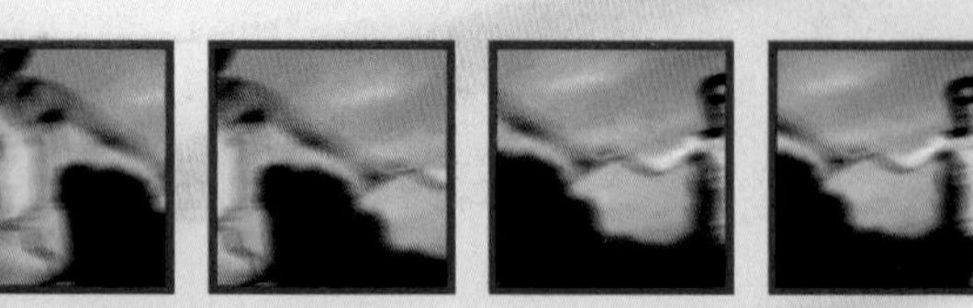

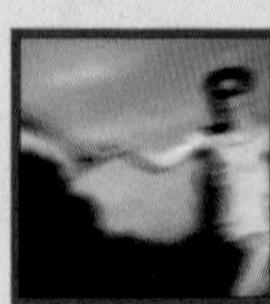